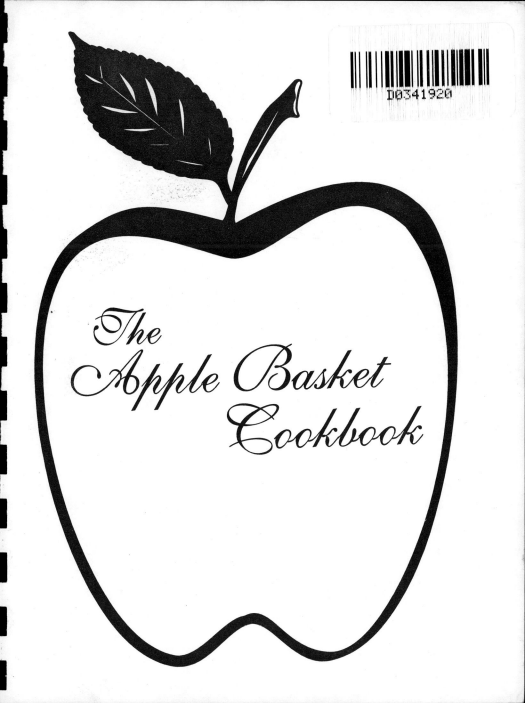

The Apple Basket Cookbook

Printed in the USA

ISBN #0-934474-77-X

APPLE VARIETIES

NAME	SEASON	COLOR	FLAVOR/ TEXTURE	EATING	PIE
Astrachan	July-Aug	Yellow/ Greenish Red	Sweet	Good	Good
Baldwin	Oct-Jan	Red/ Yellowish	Mellow	Fair	Fair
Cortland	Oct-Jan	Green/ Purple	Mild, tender	Excel.	Excel.
Delicious, Red	Sept-June	Scarlet	Sweet, crunchy	Excel.	Good
Delicious, Golden	Sept-May	Yellow	Sweet, semifirm	Excel.	Excel.
Empire	Sept-Nov	Red	Sweet, crisp	Excel.	Good
Fameuse	Sept-Nov	Red	Mild, crisp	Excel.	Fair
Granny Smith	Apr-Jul	Green	Tart, crisp	V. Good	V. Good
Gravenstein	July-Sept	Green w/red stripes	Tart, crisp	Good	Good
Ida Red	Oct	Red	Rich	Good	Good
Jonathan	Sept-Jan	Brilliant red	Tart, tender, crisp	V. Good	V. Good
Macoun	Oct-Nov	Dark red	Tart, juicy, crisp	Excel.	Good
McIntosh	Sept-June	Green to red	Slightly tart, tender, juicy	Excel.	Excel.
Newtown Pippin	Sept-June	Green to red	Slightly tart, firm	V. Good	Excel.
Northern Spy	Oct	Red	Crisp, tart	V. Good	V. Good
Rhode Island Greening	Sept-Nov	Green	Very tart, firm	Poor	Excel.

Rome Beauty	Oct-June	Red	Tart, firm, slightly dry	Good	V. Good
Stayman-Winesap	Oct-Mar	Red	Semifirm, sweet, spicy	V. Good	Good
Winesap	Oct-June	Red	Slightly tart, firm, spicy	Excel.	Good
Yellow Transparent	July-Aug	Yellow	Tart, soft	Poor	Excel.

TABLE OF CONTENTS

FAVORITE RECIPES
FROM MY COOKBOOK

Recipe Name	Page Number

APPETIZERS, BEVERAGES

LOWFAT APPLE DIP

Apple, sliced and
   cored
Equal amount of Cool
   Whip Lite and vanilla
   yogurt
Lowfat granola
Cinnamon

Mix Cool Whip and yogurt in small bowl. Dip apple slices into mixture. Sprinkle with granola and dust with cinnamon. Serves 1 or 2.

APPLE DATE SPREAD

1 (8 oz.) cream cheese
1/3 c. milk
1/2 c. heavy cream
1 c. finely chopped
   apples
1 1/2 c. finely chopped
   walnuts or
   pecans
3/4 c. finely chopped
   dates

Soften cream cheese; mix with milk and cream. Stir in remaining ingredients. Serve with Ritz crackers or nut bread. *Tastes great!*

APPLE CREAM CHEESE SPREAD

3 oz. pkg. cream
   cheese
1 Tbsp. orange juice
2 tsp. powdered sugar
1/2 c. peeled, grated
   apple

Combine cream cheese, orange juice, and sugar. Mix until smooth. Stir in apple. Use as spread for banana bread.

APPLE CHEDDAR SPREAD

¼ c. milk
1 (8 oz.) pkg. light
 Neufchatel cheese,
 softened
1 c. (4 oz.) 100%
 natural
 shredded mild
 Cheddar cheese
¼ c. finely chopped
 apple
¼ c. finely chopped
 walnuts
1 Tbsp. sugar
¼ tsp. cinnamon

Gradually add milk to Neufchatel cheese, mixing until well blended. Add remaining ingredients, mixing at medium speed on electric mixer until well blended. Chill. Serve with crackers.

APPLE NUT LOG

1 (8 oz.) pkg. cream
 cheese, softened
1 Tbsp. apple juice
½ tsp. ground nutmeg
1 tsp. fresh lemon
 juice
1 c. chopped tart
 apples
1 c. chopped pecans

Combine cream cheese, apple juice, and nutmeg in mixer bowl; blend until smooth. Pour lemon juice over chopped apples and add to the creamed cheese mixture. Gently fold in ¾ cup of the pecans, then shape into a 6 inch log and roll in the remaining chopped nuts. Wrap in plastic and refrigerate until ready to serve. Slice and serve on crackers.

Makes a different type party snack.

APPLE CHEDDAR CANAPES

7 to 9 slices rye bread
1 large Granny Smith
   apple, peeled,
   cored, and coarsely
   grated
1 c. coarsely grated
   extra sharp Cheddar
   cheese
3 Tbsp. mayonnaise
1 Tbsp. honey
1 tsp. Dijon mustard
¼ tsp. caraway seeds
Freshly ground pepper
   to taste

Cut out 3 or 4 rounds from each slice of bread, using a 2 inch round cutter. On a baking sheet, toast the rounds under a preheated broiler, turning once until golden. In a bowl, combine the apple, Cheddar cheese, mayonnaise, honey, mustard, caraway seeds, and pepper. Spread each toast with a scant teaspoon and broil for approximately 2 minutes. Makes approximately 28 pieces, serving 6 to 8 people.

SAUSAGE-APPLE BALLS

1 lb. pork sausage
3 c. biscuit mix
1 c. raisins, chopped
1 c. grated, unpeeled
   apple
½ c. chopped walnuts
½ tsp. apple pie spice

Combine all ingredients, mixing well. Shape into 1 inch balls. Place on ungreased baking sheets; bake at 350° for 20 minutes or until lightly browned. Yield: About 4½ dozen.

3

TEXAS WINGS

Sauce:
1 c. apple juice
⅓ c. lime juice
¾ c. Louisiana hot
  sauce
1 tsp. Worcestershire
  sauce
1 tsp. celery seed
1 tsp. white pepper
½ tsp. Tabasco sauce
1 tsp. salt
1 tsp. cornstarch

Chicken:
20 chicken drumettes
2 c. all-purpose flour
2 tsp. salt
2 tsp. black pepper
1 tsp. paprika

Combine all ingredients, except water and cornstarch, in a pan and bring to a boil. Combine water and cornstarch in a separate bowl, then stir into boiling liquid. Cook for 5 minutes, stirring constantly. Set aside, but keep warm. Combine flour with salt, pepper, and paprika; mix to distribute seasonings. Dust the chicken drumettes in the seasoned flour. Deep-fry until golden brown. Place fried drumettes in a bowl and ladle sauce over them. Toss to coat. Remove chicken from sauce and serve with Ranch dressing.

SWEET AND SOUR SMOKIES

1 c. apple jelly
1 c. mustard
1 pkg. little cocktail
  smokies

Bring jelly and mustard to boil. Add smokies. Simmer 20 minutes.

HOT CIDER FLOAT

Apple cider, heated
Vanilla ice cream
Cinnamon

For each serving, fill glass or mug ⅔ full of warm cider. Top with 2 small scoops ice cream. Sprinkle with cinnamon.

CREAMY STRAWBERRY AND APPLE SHAKE

2 c. fresh or thawed
   strawberries
1 c. plain nonfat
   yogurt
2½ c. unsweetened
   apple juice,
   chilled
1 fresh strawberry,
   halved for
   garnish
Mint sprig

In a blender, process strawberries, yogurt, and apple juice 1 minute or until smooth. Pour into a glass and garnish with sliced berry and mint sprig. Makes 2 servings.

WAKE UP DRINK

1 egg or ⅓ to ½ c.
   yogurt
1 banana
1 c. orange juice
1 apple, cored and
   chopped

Put in blender. Blend. Serves 6.

Note: Leave apple unpeeled.

SPICED APPLE CIDER

1 gal. apple cider
1 gal. cranberry juice
2 c. brown sugar
12 cloves
7 cinnamon sticks

Pour cider and cranberry juice into a 35 cup coffee maker. Place brown sugar, cloves, and cinnamon sticks into basket and put into coffee maker. Let perk until hot. Serve in coffee mugs with a cinnamon stick.

5

SLUSH

1 (12 oz.) can frozen
   apple juice
2 (12 oz.) cans frozen
   orange juice
1 large can pineapple
   juice
1 (12 oz.) can frozen
   lemonade
6 large bananas
½ c. honey
4 c. water

Blend bananas, honey, and water. Add to the apple juice, orange juice, pineapple juice, and frozen lemonade mixture in a 5 quart ice cream pail and freeze. To use, put 1 ice cream scoop in a glass and fill with 7-Up.

Can also be served from a punch bowl.

SWING SET PUNCH

1 pt. cranberry juice
1 qt. apple juice
12 oz. frozen
   lemonade
   concentrate
6 oz. frozen pineapple
   concentrate
2 (28 oz.) bottles
   lemon-lime soda

Combine juices and stir. Add soda. Serve over ice. *Nice and tangy!*

PARTY PUNCH

1 qt. orange juice
1 qt. pineapple juice
1 qt. apple juice
2 qt. ginger ale
Ice or lime or orange
   sherbet

Mix juices at least 3 hours before the party to mix up the flavors. Pour in ginger ale just before you serve it. Pour over ice or sherbet. Serves about 30.

6

MERRY BREW

½ c. firmly packed
  brown sugar
¼ tsp. salt
2 sticks cinnamon
1 Tbsp. whole cloves
½ tsp. whole allspice
1 c. water
2 qt. apple juice
1 lemon, thinly sliced
1 orange, thinly sliced

Combine sugar, salt, spices, and water in a small saucepan; bring to a boil. Reduce heat and simmer 10 minutes. Combine apple juice and fruit slices in a large saucepan. Heat gently. Strain hot spice liquid into apple juice and serve warm. Yield: 2 quarts.

SWEET AND SASSY SIPPER

3 c. apple juice
1 c. water
½ (6 oz.) can (⅓ c.)
  frozen
  lemonade
  concentrate
Ice cubes

In a pitcher, combine apple juice, water, and lemonade concentrate. Stir gently and chill. Pour over ice cubes and serve.

HONEY APPLE TEA

6 tea bags
3 c. boiling water
Lemon slices
3 c. apple juice
⅓ c. honey

In a 2 quart pot, brew tea bags in boiling water. Remove tea bags; add honey and apple juice. Simmer until hot. Ladle into cups and garnish with lemon slices. Makes 6 to 8 servings.

7

WASSAIL BOWL WITH BAKED APPLES

3 large cooking
  apples, cored
1 gal. apple cider
6 whole cloves
2 tsp. ground nutmeg
1 (6 oz.) can frozen
  lemonade
  concentrate
1 (6 oz.) can frozen
  orange juice
  concentrate
1 c. packed brown
  sugar
Sugar
Short cinnamon sticks

Preheat oven to 350°. Cut apples in halves crosswise and place, cut side down, in 13x9 inch baking dish. Bake 25 minutes or until the apple halves are fork-tender.

Meanwhile, in covered 6 quart saucepan over low heat, simmer 2 cups apple cider, cloves, and nutmeg 10 minutes. Add remaining apple cider, undiluted lemonade and orange juice concentrates, and brown sugar; heat until hot, but not boiling, stirring occasionally. Pour hot cider mixture from saucepan into heated large punch bowl. Float apples, skin side up, in punch; sprinkle tops with a little sugar.

To serve, ladle about ½ cup of hot punch into each punch cup; add a short cinnamon stick to each serving.

SOUPS, SALADS

APPLEY CHEESE SOUP

½ c. pared, chopped
  apples
¼ c. chopped onion
½ c. finely chopped
  carrots and
  celery
½ c. butter or
  margarine
¼ c. flour
2 c. apple juice
2 c. milk
½ lb. grated sharp
  Cheddar cheese
1 c. minced, cooked
  ham

In large saucepan, over medium heat, saute onions, carrots, celery, apples, and ham in butter until vegetables are cooked tender. Sprinkle in flour and stir until smooth. Add apple juice and milk. Continue cooking to a boil. Add cheese and stir over medium heat until cheese melts. Add salt and pepper to taste if desired.

Optional: Garnish with spoonful of sour cream and thin apple slice.

CREAMY APPLE SOUP

1 c. celery, diced
1 c. chopped onion
2 c. unpeeled, ½ inch
  apple chunks
3 Tbsp. butter
4 c. chicken broth
½ c. nonfat dry milk
  powder
Salt and pepper to
  taste

Saute celery, onions, and apple chunks in butter until tender. Add broth; cover and simmer over very low heat 10 minutes. Press through sieve or food mill. Return to saucepan. Stir in milk powder, salt, and pepper. Heat through. Garnish with apple wedges.

ACORN SQUASH AND APPLE SOUP

2 medium acorn
   squash, seeded
   and halved
3 c. degreased chicken
   stock or canned
2 tart green apples (2
   c.), cored,
   seeded, and
   chopped
½ c. chopped onion
1 c. unsweetened
   apple juice
2 tsp. fresh ginger
   root, peeled and
   grated
½ tsp. salt (omit if
   using canned
   stock)
1 Tbsp. fresh lemon
   juice
White pepper to taste
Yogurt or sour cream
   and chives
   (garnish)

Cook squash and remove pulp. Combine ½ cup stock, apples, and onion in heavy medium saucepan. Cover and cook over low heat for 10 minutes. Add squash pulp, remaining stock, apple juice, ginger, and salt. Cover and simmer until ingredients are very tender, about 20 minutes. Puree soup in batches in blender or processor. Strain through sieve into clean saucepan, pressing puree with back of spoon. Reheat soup gently. Season with salt and generous amount of pepper. Ladle into bowls. Garnish with yogurt or sour cream and chives.

10

SPICY BEEF STEW

2 lb. lean beef stew
   meat
1½ tsp. sugar
1 tsp. salt
⅔ tsp. whole allspice
1 bay leaf
1 c. apple cider
1 (10½ oz.) can beef
   broth
4 carrots, peeled and
   cut in large
   chunks
4 small onions,
   quartered
2 Tbsp. cornstarch
½ c. water

Trim fat from meat and add to hot heavy casserole to grease bottom. Remove pieces and discard. Cut meat in 2 inch cubes and brown quickly. Sprinkle sugar over meat and brown until sugar caramelizes, giving rich brown color. Add salt, allspice, bay leaf, cider, and beef broth. Bring to boiling and add carrots and onions. Return to simmer. Cover and place in oven at 350° for 2 to 2½ hours (until meat is tender). Stir cornstarch into water. Stir mixture into stew. Cook until thickened. Flavor improves if served following day.

CIDER STEW

2 lb. boneless stew
   meat
2 Tbsp. cooking oil
3 Tbsp. flour
¼ tsp. thyme
2 c. apple cider
½ c. water
2 Tbsp. vinegar
3 medium potatoes,
   quartered
4 carrots
1 small onion
1 c. celery

Brown meat in flour, thyme, and oil. Simmer meat for 2 hours in apple cider, water, and vinegar. Add potatoes, carrots, onion, and celery. Cook until tender.

MEAL-IN-A-BOWL SOUP

1 Tbsp. vegetable oil
1½ lb. boneless pork,
   cut into ¾ inch
   pieces
¾ c. apple juice
¼ tsp. ground black
   pepper
½ tsp. caraway seed
2 medium red
   potatoes, cut into
   chunks
2 c. coarsely chopped
   cabbage
2 carrots, diagonally
   sliced
2 (10¾ oz.) cans
   condensed
   cream of celery soup
2 soup cans milk

1. In 4 quart saucepan over medium heat in hot oil, cook pork until browned on all sides.
2. Add juice, pepper, and caraway. Heat to boiling. Reduce heat to low. Cover; simmer 20 minutes, stirring occasionally.
3. Add potatoes. Cover; cook 10 minutes. Add cabbage and carrots. Cover; cook 15 minutes or until vegetables are tender.

12

APPLE AMBROSIA

1 (20 oz.) can
  pineapple
  chunks
1 small can mandarin
  orange sections
1 c. shredded coconut
1 c. small
  marshmallows
12 maraschino
  cherries, sliced
1 banana, sliced
1 unpeeled apple,
  finely diced
1 Tbsp. juice from
  each - oranges,
  pineapple, and
  cherries (3 Tbsp.
  total)
1 pt. sour cream (or 1
  pt. Cool Whip)

Mix gently; chill well in covered container. Serves 7 to 8.

APPLESAUCE-RASPBERRY SALAD

1 (3 oz.) pkg.
  raspberry
  gelatin
1 c. boiling water
1 (10 oz.) pkg. frozen
  raspberries
1 c. applesauce
1 c. dairy sour cream
1 c. miniature
  marshmallows

Dissolve gelatin in boiling water. Add frozen raspberries and stir until thawed. Stir in applesauce. Pour in 10x6 inch dish. Chill until set. Combine sour cream and marshmallows. Spread on top of gelatin. Cover and chill until set.

13

RED HOT APPLESAUCE JELLO

1 c. water
1 c. red hots
2 c. applesauce
1 large pkg. any flavor
   red jello

Put red hots and water in pan and on low heat. Stir constantly until red hots are totally dissolved. Remove from heat and add jello. Stir until jello is dissolved and add applesauce. Stir until mixed well. Pour into bowl and refrigerate until set.

Best if made the day before. Serve plain or with Cool Whip.

APPLESAUCE-CREAM CHEESE SALAD

1 c. red hots
1 pkg. lemon jello
2 pkg. cream cheese
1 c. hot water
16 oz. applesauce
½ c. nuts
Pinch of salt

Mix red hots, water, jello, and applesauce. Pour ½ of the mix in a dish to cool and set. Add enough cream to the cheese to spread. Add nuts and salt. Spread over first mixture and cool. Add second half of the first mix. Chill to set firmly.

CARAMEL APPLE SALAD

1 c. sugar
2 Tbsp. flour
2 eggs, slightly beaten
2 Tbsp. lemon juice
1 (20 oz.) can crushed
   pineapple,
   drained
6 to 8 apples, diced
   (unpeeled)
1 (12 oz.) pkg. Cool
   Whip
2 c. dry roasted
   peanuts,
   chopped

Cook sugar, flour, eggs, and lemon juice until thick. Cool. Combine pineapple and Cool Whip. Stir in apples and 1½ cups peanuts, then stir in the cooled mixture. Top with remaining crushed peanuts.

14

SUNFLOWER WALDORF SALAD

2 small apples, cored
  and chopped
  (1½ c.)
¼ c. seedless green
  grapes, halved
¼ c. chopped celery
⅓ c. sunflower nuts
¼ c. plain yogurt
1 large banana, sliced
Lettuce leaves

In mixing bowl, toss together apples, grapes, celery, and sunflower nuts. Fold in yogurt and banana. Serve on individual lettuce-lined salad plates. Garnish with additional banana slices if desired. Makes 3 or 4 servings.

Lemon or apple-flavored yogurt may be substituted for plain yogurt.

APPLE WALNUT GELATIN

¼ c. unsweetened
  chilled apple
  juice
1 pkg. unflavored
  gelatin
1¾ c. unsweetened
  apple juice

Filling:
½ c. chopped walnuts
½ c. chopped apple

Pour chilled apple juice in a small bowl and sprinkle over it the unflavored gelatin. Mix and allow to set 2 to 3 minutes to soften. Heat rest of apple juice to a boil. Mix together gelatin mixture and boiling apple juice; cool and refrigerate. When mixture reaches the consistency of unbeaten egg whites, stir in apple and walnuts. Return to refrigerator and chill. Serve with a garnish of whip cream.

CRANAPPLE CREAM CHEESE SALAD

1 (6 oz.) pkg. cherry
gelatin
2 c. boiling water
2 large apples, peeled
and grated
1½ c. chopped pecans
or pecan pieces
2 c. cooked or 1 (16
oz.) can whole
cranberry sauce
Cream Cheese
Topping (recipe follows)
Additional pecans

Cream Cheese
Topping:
1 (8 oz.) pkg. cream
cheese, softened
1 c. powdered sugar
1 (1 lb. 4 oz.) can
crushed
pineapple, drained
1 (1.4 oz.) env.
whipped topping mix
½ c. cold milk
1 tsp. vanilla

Dissolve cherry gelatin in boiling water. Cool slightly. Add apples, chopped pecans, and cranberry sauce. Turn into 13x9 inch glass baking dish and refrigerate until firm. Spoon Cream Cheese Topping over top, spreading evenly. Sprinkle with additional pecans, about ¼ cup chopped, or garnish with pecan halves if desired. Cover and chill overnight until set. Makes about 12 servings.

Cream Cheese Topping: Blend cream cheese and ½ cup powdered sugar until smooth. Mix in crushed pineapple. Whip topping mix with cold milk until stiff. Stir in remaining powdered sugar and vanilla. Gradually add to cream cheese mixture.

Note: Instead of using reconstituted whipped topping mix, 2 cups of frozen whipped topping (omit sugar, not vanilla) may be used.

EGGNOG FRUIT SALAD

1 c. eggnog, chilled
1 (2 oz.) env. dessert
  topping
¼ tsp. ground nutmeg
1 (16 oz.) can sliced
  peaches,
  drained
1 (13 oz.) can
  pineapple
  tidbits, drained
1 medium unpared
  apple, cored and
  chopped
¼ c. maraschino
  cherries,
  drained and halved
⅓ c. chopped walnuts

In small mixer bowl, combine eggnog, dessert topping mix, and nutmeg. Beat at high speed of electric mixer about 5 minutes. Combine fruits and nuts; fold in eggnog mixture. Cover and chill several hours. Makes 6 to 8 servings.

APPLE SNOW SALAD

1 c. crushed pineapple
2 beaten eggs
½ c. sugar
Dash of salt
3 Tbsp. lemon juice
3 c. finely diced,
  unpeeled apple
½ c. finely diced celery
1 c. heavy cream,
  whipped

Drain pineapple and reserve juice. Add water to juice to make ½ cup. Combine eggs, sugar, salt, lemon juice, and pineapple juice. Cook over low heat, stirring constantly until thick. Chill. Fold in pineapple, apple, celery, and the whipped cream. Pour into 2 quart refrigerator dish (or dish of your choice). Freeze firm. Cut in squares and trim with fans of apple slices. Makes 10 to 12 servings.

APPLE SLAW

1 head green cabbage
2 lb. apples
⅓ c. ReaLemon
1 c. brown sugar
1 tsp. dry mustard
1 Tbsp. celery seed
1 c. mayonnaise
Salt and pepper to
taste

Shred the cabbage; wash and slice the apples. Don't bother to peel the apples as skin adds flavor and color. Toss the slices in lemon juice so they won't turn brown. Add the sugar, celery seed, and mustard; combine with the cabbage and apples. Add the mayonnaise and the salad will shrink like magic. Salt and pepper to taste. Feeds a crowd - at least 12.

SPINACH SALAD WITH APPLE AND BACON

¼ c. salad oil
3 Tbsp. red wine
vinegar
1 tsp. sugar
½ tsp. prepared
mustard
Salt and freshly
ground pepper
5 slices bacon
1 c. slivered almonds
1 lb. fresh spinach,
torn into bite-
size pieces
2 unpeeled red apples,
cored and
coarsely chopped

Combine oil, vinegar, sugar, mustard, salt, and pepper in jar with tight lid; shake well and refrigerate. Cook bacon; drain well and crumble. Discard all but 1 tablespoon bacon fat. Toast almonds in fat. Combine spinach, bacon, apple, and almonds. Just before serving, pour dressing over and toss.

APPLE TUNA SALAD

1 (7 oz.) can tuna,
   drained
2 c. sliced celery
1 Tbsp. minced onion
¼ c. minced green
   peppers
½ c. peanuts
1 tsp. salt
¼ tsp. pepper
2 apples, cored
2 Tbsp. lemon juice
½ c. mayonnaise
⅓ c. sour cream
Crisp salad greens,
   refrigerated 1
   hour

Flake tuna into a bowl; add celery, onion, green pepper, peanuts, salt, and pepper. Cube the apples. Sprinkle lemon juice over them to keep apples from darkening. Add to tuna fish. Combine mayonnaise and sour cream. Carefully blend into tuna mixture. Cover and refrigerate. Serve with salad greens.

APPLE POTATO SALAD

4 medium red
   potatoes
2 boiled eggs
1 heaping Tbsp. pickle
   relish
1 small onion, finely
   chopped
   (optional)
½ apple, chopped into
   ½ inch cubes
1 tsp. mustard
2 heaping Tbsp.
   mayonnaise

Peel potatoes and wash thoroughly. Cut into ½ inch cubes. In pan, cover the potatoes with salted water. Bring to boil and cook over medium heat for 20 minutes or until potatoes are tender, but firm. Do not let them boil dry. Drain and cool for 10 minutes. To the potatoes, add the rest of ingredients. Mix well and serve warm or chilled. Makes 4 servings.

19

CAULIFLOWER AND BROCCOLI SALAD

1 small head
  cauliflower,
  broken in pieces
1 bunch broccoli,
  broken in pieces
1 c. Cheddar cheese
  (bite-size)
2 or 3 red apples
  (unpeeled), cut
  in pieces
½ c. mayonnaise
1 pkg. Ranch dressing
½ c. sour cream
1 c. milk
½ c. sunflower seeds

Mix first 4 ingredients in bowl. Mix dry dressing with mayonnaise, milk, and sour cream. Toss with vegetables and cheese. Before serving, add sunflower seeds. Refrigerate.

ROSY APPLESAUCE

5 to 6 lb. (15 to 20)
  red-skinned
  apples
1 c. water
1 c. sugar
½ c. light brown sugar
1 tsp. cinnamon
  (optional)

Wash apples; remove bud and stem areas. Do not peel or core. Cut into quarters. Place apples into a 5-quart saucepan with water; bring to a boil, and simmer for 30 to 40 minutes or until the pulp softens and separates from the peel. Stir occasionally. Press through a food mill or a colander. Add sugar and cinnamon to the warm applesauce and allow to stand until cool enough to eat. Serve warm or chilled. Yield: 6 to 8 cups.

VEGETABLES

CRANBERRY-APPLE SWEET POTATOES

5 to 6 medium sweet
potatoes,
cooked and peeled,
or 2 (18 oz.) cans,
drained and cut into
bite-size pieces
1 (21 oz.) can apple
pie filling
1 (8 oz.) can whole
cranberry sauce
2 Tbsp. apricot
preserves
2 Tbsp. orange
marmalade

Spread pie filling in 8x8x2 inch baking dish. Arrange sweet potatoes on top. In small mixing bowl, stir together cranberry sauce, preserves, and marmalade. Spoon over sweet potatoes. Bake, uncovered, at 350° for 20 to 25 minutes.

APPLE AND YAM CASSEROLE

21 oz. can apple pie
filling
2 (17 oz.) cans whole
sweet potatoes,
drained
3 Tbsp. butter
Nutmeg
Chopped nuts

Preheat oven to 325°. Combine apple pie filling and sweet potatoes. Place in buttered casserole, dot with butter, and sprinkle with nutmeg and nuts. Bake 30 minutes or until bubbly.

21

BUTTERNUT SQUASH AND APPLE CASSEROLE

3 c. cooked, mashed
  butternut
  squash
2 Tbsp. butter or
  margarine,
  melted
1 Tbsp. brown sugar
¼ tsp. salt
1 Tbsp. butter or
  margarine
6 c. peeled, chopped
  apple
¼ c. sugar
1½ c. corn flakes,
  coarsely
  crushed
½ c. chopped pecans
½ c. firmly packed
  brown sugar
2 Tbsp. butter or
  margarine,
  melted

Combine first 4 ingredients, stirring well; set aside. Melt 1 tablespoon butter in a large skillet; add apples and sugar. Cover and simmer 8 to 10 minutes or until tender. Drain off excess liquid. Stir apples into squash mixture. Spoon into a lightly greased 2 quart casserole. Combine remaining ingredients, stirring well. Sprinkle over squash. Bake at 350° for 20 minutes or until thoroughly heated.

CIDER BAKED ACORN SQUASH

2 medium acorn
  squash
½ c. apple cider
¼ c. packed brown
  sugar
½ tsp. salt
⅛ tsp. cinnamon
⅛ tsp. mace (optional)

Slice squash in 1 inch circles and remove seeds. Place squash in 15x10x1 inch baking pan. Pour cider over squash. Combine all the rest of the ingredients and sprinkle on top of squash. Cover with foil. Bake at 325° for 45 minutes or until squash is tender. Serves 6.

APPLE ONION BAKE

6 to 8 large tart apples
1 large onion, sliced
  thin
5 Tbsp. butter or
  margarine
2 Tbsp. sugar
2 Tbsp. cinnamon
1 c. apple juice or
  apple cider
30 to 40 Ritz crackers,
  crushed

Saute onion in 2 tablespoons butter until golden; set aside. Mix sugar and cinnamon; set aside. Melt 3 tablespoons butter in large saucepan. Saute apples until tender, about 5 minutes. Butter 1½ quart casserole dish. Spoon half of apples evenly on bottom of casserole dish. Spread half of the onions over apples. Sprinkle with half of sugar mixture. Sprinkle with half of Ritz crackers. Repeat all layers. Dot with remaining butter. Pour in apple juice or cider. Bake at 325° for 1 hour until bubbly. Serves 6 to 8.

SWEET GLAZED APPLE AND CARROTS

6 medium carrots,
  sliced, or 3 c.
  frozen
1 medium apple,
  cored and sliced
2 Tbsp. brown sugar
2 Tbsp. margarine or
  butter
1 Tbsp. lemon juice

In medium saucepan, cook the fresh carrots, covered, in boiling salt water about 15 minutes or until tender (or cooked frozen carrots according to package directions). Drain thoroughly. Add apple, brown sugar, margarine, and lemon juice to carrots in saucepan; mix well. Cover and cook about 5 minutes or until apple is tender.

SAUERKRAUT

2 lb. bag sauerkraut
1 large apple, peeled
   and grated
1 onion, diced fine
¼ c. water (approx.)
1 tsp. caraway seed (or
   to taste)
2 Tbsp. brown sugar
   (adjust to taste)
1 Tbsp. flour

Drain and rinse sauerkraut. Place sauerkraut and next 5 ingredients in pan. Heat to boiling. Add flour, stirring thoroughly. Reduce heat and simmer 20 minutes.

SCALLOPED APPLES AND CABBAGE

1 medium apple,
   sliced thin
3 c. shredded cabbage
1 tsp. salt
1 tsp. sugar
½ c. bread crumbs
2 Tbsp. butter
¼ c. water

In a covered casserole, alternate layers of cabbage and apples. Season each layer with salt and sugar. Add water. Put crumbs on top and dot with butter. Bake in moderately hot oven about 40 minutes until apples are tender. Remove cover for final 10 minutes of baking to brown crumbs.

MAIN DISHES

APPLE STUFFED PORK CHOPS

1 medium apple,
  peeled, cored,
  and diced
1 small onion,
  chopped
½ c. raisins
1 tsp. salt
2 c. fresh bread
  crumbs
¼ tsp. pepper
¼ tsp. sage
3 Tbsp. melted butter
6 thick pork chops
3 Tbsp. vegetable oil

Combine apple, onion, salt, bread crumbs, pepper, sage, and butter. Add water if mixture appears too dry. Cut a deep pocket into the side of each pork chop and stuff with the apple dressing. Secure with a toothpick.

In large skillet, brown the stuffed chops on each side in the oil. Place chops in shallow ovenproof casserole and arrange the remaining dressing around the chops. Bake in preheated 350° oven for about 1 hour. Last 5 minutes, saute lightly the raisins and add to casserole. Serves 4 to 6 people.

HONEY APPLE CHOPS

4 (1½ inch) boneless
  loin chops
1½ c. apple cider
¼ c. lemon juice
¼ c. soy sauce
2 Tbsp. honey
1 clove garlic, minced
¼ tsp. pepper

Combine all ingredients, except chops; mix well. Place chops in a shallow dish; pour marinade over chops. Cover and refrigerate 4 to 24 hours. Prepare covered grill with drip pan in center, banked by medium-hot coals. Grill chops for 12 to 15 minutes, turning once and basting occasionally with marinade. Serves 4.

APPLE GLAZED PORK CHOPS

¼ c. flour
½ tsp. salt
½ tsp. dry mustard
⅛ tsp. pepper
2 lb. pork chops
2 Tbsp. butter or
  margarine
2 Tbsp. flour
2 Tbsp. brown sugar
1½ c. apple juice
2 apples, peeled and
  sliced
⅓ c. raisins
½ tsp. cinnamon

Combine ¼ cup flour, salt, mustard, and pepper. Coat pork chops in flour mixture; brown in margarine. Remove chops; stir 2 tablespoons flour and brown sugar into drippings to make a thick paste. Gradually stir in apple juice; cook and stir until thickened.

Place chops in 2 quart casserole. Arrange apple slices and raisins over pork chops; cover with apple juice mixture. Sprinkle with cinnamon. Cover and bake at 350° for 1 hour. Makes 4 servings.

APPLE-GINGER PORK TENDERLOIN

1 Tbsp. flour
1¼ tsp. garlic salt
1 tsp. ginger
1¼ lb. pork tenderloin
¼ c. vegetable oil
1 Tbsp. cornstarch
1 Tbsp. water
1¼ c. apple juice
Fresh parsley and
  apple wedges
  (optional)

Combine flour, garlic salt, and ginger. Dredge tenderloin in flour mixture. Cook tenderloin, uncovered, in hot oil in a skillet over low heat for 10 minutes, turning occasionally. Cover and cook an additional 35 minutes. Combine cornstarch and water in a small saucepan, stirring until smooth. Stir in apple juice. Bring to a boil and cook 1 minute or until thick, stirring constantly. Serve sauce over sliced tenderloin. Garnish with parsley and apple wedges if desired.

APPLE BASTED HONEY BAKED HAM

**10 to 12 lb. ready-to-
  eat bone-in ham
3 Tbsp. Dijon mustard
1 c. brown sugar
½ c. honey
1 tsp. cinnamon
1½ c. apple juice**

Remove the layer of skin from ham, leaving a thin layer of fat to keep the meat juicy while baking. Score the surface of the ham in a diamond pattern, without cutting into the meat. Place a whole clove in the center of half the diamonds. Place ham in roasting pan and brush top with mustard. Combine sugar, honey, and cinnamon; heat over medium temperature, about 2 minutes until mixture will pour, but not thin. Spread over ham. Pour apple juice in bottom of roasting pan and bake at 325° for 1½ hours. Baste every half hour using juices in the pan.

HAM AND APPLE PITAS

**2 cans (4½ oz.) light
  deviled ham
1 large Delicious
  apple, chopped
½ c. chopped pecans
½ c. diced celery
3 whole wheat pocket
  pita bread (halves)
Leafy lettuce**

In medium bowl, combine all ingredients, except lettuce and bread. Line each pocket with lettuce leaves and spoon ½ cup ham mixture between lettuce.

COUNTRY APPLE AND KRAUT DINNER

**1 (2 lb.) smoked pork
  butt
1 lb. can sauerkraut
2 c. apple juice
1 large bay leaf
6 medium potatoes
6 small onions
6 carrots, quartered**

Place pork butt in 5 quart Dutch oven; add sauerkraut, apple juice, and bay leaf. Cover and simmer 1 hour. Add remaining ingredients; simmer, covered, 45 minutes more or until tender. Remove to serving platter. Serve with applesauce and biscuits. Serves 6.

27

SAVORY KIELBASA SKILLET

2 medium red cooking apples
2 Tbsp. butter or margarine
1 small onion, diced
1 small red cabbage, shredded (about 6 c.)
½ c. apple juice
1 Tbsp. sugar
3 Tbsp. red wine vinegar
¼ tsp. pepper
Pinch of salt
1 lb. kielbasa, sliced 1 inch

Peel, core, and dice 1 apple. Cook onion until tender in 10 inch skillet in hot butter or margarine. Add diced apple, cabbage, apple juice, sugar, vinegar, salt, and pepper. Heat to boiling. Reduce heat to low, cover, and simmer 15 minutes, stirring occasionally. Add kielbasa to mixture over high heat; heat to boiling. Reduce to low and simmer 15 minutes longer or until sausage is heated through. Core, but don't peel, remaining apple. Cut into wedges and add to skillet; heat through.

APPLE-SAUSAGE BRUNCH PIZZA

1 lb. bulk pork sausage
2 c. Bisquick baking mix
½ c. cold water
½ c. brown sugar
2 Tbsp. flour
1 tsp. cinnamon
½ c. apple juice
2 medium apples, cut into ½ inch pieces

Cook and stir sausage until brown; drain well. Mix baking mix and water until soft dough forms. Roll or pat dough into 12 inch circle on ungreased cookie sheet; pinch edge of circle, forming ½ inch rim. Mix brown sugar, flour, cinnamon, and apple juice in saucepan. Heat to boiling, stirring constantly. Boil and stir 1 minute. Stir in sausage and apples. Spoon onto dough. Bake until crust is golden brown (at 425° for 25 to 30 minutes). Makes 8 slices.

28

APPLE HERBED CHICKEN

6 boned and skinned
   whole chicken
   breasts
3 Tbsp. butter
¾ tsp. Bon Appetit
1 tsp. lemon juice
⅛ tsp. ground white
   pepper
½ tsp. parsley flakes
½ tsp. rosemary
   leaves, crushed
1 Tbsp. freeze-dried
   chopped chives
½ c. cider or apple
   juice
½ c. heavy cream

In large skillet, brown chicken in butter over low heat about 10 minutes. Add remaining ingredients, except heavy cream. Cover and simmer 20 minutes or until chicken is tender. Remove chicken and keep warm. Add cream to pan liquid; stir and heat through. Spoon over chicken and serve with wild rice mix.

CHICKEN WITH APPLES AND ONIONS

6 skinless chicken
   breast halves
1 c. sliced onion
1 Tbsp. olive oil
2 c. sliced tart apples
1 Tbsp. margarine
1½ c. apple juice
2 Tbsp. honey
½ to 1 tsp. salt

Preheat oven to 350°. Place chicken breasts in a shallow baking pan. In a skillet, saute onions in olive oil until tender. Add apples and saute for 1 more minute. Pour onions and apples over chicken. Melt margarine in a small saucepan. Combine apple juice, honey, salt, and margarine; pour over chicken and vegetables. Bake for 45 minutes or until chicken is cooked through. Serves 6.

May want to double marinade and thicken with cornstarch or flour to make a thicker gravy for the chicken or for potatoes, rice, or other veggies.

SUNDAY CHICKEN

2 Tbsp. butter
3 tsp. curry powder
1 medium apple,
  chopped fine
2½ to 3 lb. fryer (6
  good sized)
  chicken breasts
1 can condensed
  cream of
  mushroom soup
1 c. evaporated milk
Salt
Paprika

Melt butter in saucepan. Saute in curry powder apple and onion. Cook until onion is transparent, then add soup and milk. Salt and paprika chicken and spread it out in one layer in a shallow buttered baking pan. Pour the sauce over chicken. Bake, uncovered, at 350° for about 1½ hours or until chicken is tender.

APPLE CIDER CHICKEN

4 chicken breasts
1 can cream of chicken
  soup
1 Tbsp. plus 1 tsp.
  Worcestershire
¾ tsp. salt
⅓ c. chopped onion
1 clove garlic, minced
1 can mushrooms
¾ c. apple cider
Paprika

Heat oven to 350°. Have on hand a 13x9 inch pan. Blend all. Pour over chicken. Sprinkle generously with paprika. Bake 1½ to 2 hours. Baste with sauce during baking. After 1 hour, sprinkle again with paprika.

APPLE HONEY GLAZED HENS

2 Cornish hens
2 c. apple cider
¼ tsp. ground ginger
2 Tbsp. honey
3 Tbsp. butter
Salt and pepper to
    taste

Apple Stuffing:
1 pkg. stuffing mix
2 diced apples
1 c. chopped celery
½ c. chopped walnuts
Pinch of ground
    nutmeg

Mix cider and ginger; boil and reduce to ¼ cup. Stir in honey and butter. Season hens with salt and pepper. Stuff hens with apple stuffing. Tie legs together, wings back. Put hens in shallow roasting pan. Pour glaze over hens. Bake at 375° for 55 to 60 minutes.

APPLE SPICED BRISKET

1 Tbsp. flour
3 to 4 lb. beef brisket
    (first cut, flat
    half, boneless)
1 tsp. salt
1½ c. apple juice
¼ c. honey
1 tsp. ground
    cinnamon
1 tsp. ground ginger
1 tsp. ground nutmeg
2 Tbsp. flour
¼ c. raisins
1 apple, sliced

Preheat oven to 325°. Shake 1 tablespoon flour in a large size (14x20 inches) oven cooking bag and place in 13x9x2 inch baking pan. Prick brisket with fork on both sides; sprinkle with salt. Place brisket, fat side up, in bag. Combine apple juice, honey, and spices; pour over brisket. Close bag with nylon tie; make 6 (½ inch) slices in top. Bake 2 to 2½ hours or until tender.

In medium saucepan, dissolve 2 tablespoons flour in small amount of cooking liquid from bag. Stir in remaining cooking liquid, raisins, and apple slices. Bring to a boil. Boil and stir 1 to 2 minutes to form light gravy. Thinly slice brisket diagonally across grain. Serve with apple raisin gravy. Makes 6 to 8 servings.

31

BAKED CHICKEN BARBECUE

8 chicken breast
  halves or 8 legs
  (or 4 of each)
Salt and pepper to
  taste
½ c. melted butter
1½ c. chili sauce
⅓ c. water
2 medium onions,
  sliced
⅓ c. brown sugar
½ c. raisins
2 tsp. Worcestershire
  sauce
6 apples, sliced

Rub chicken with salt and pepper. Brush with butter and broil lightly on both sides. Combine chili sauce, water, onions, sugar, raisins, and Worcestershire sauce. Pour over chicken in a shallow baking pan; cover with foil. Bake at 325° for about 50 minutes, or until chicken is cooked through. Add apples during the last half hour of baking time. Yield: 6 to 8 servings.

Note: This dish can be prepared in advance, omitting the apples, and refrigerated. Add the apples when reheating.

SWEET AND SOUR ROAST

½ c. vinegar
½ c. apple juice
½ c. chili sauce
2 Tbsp. brown sugar
1 tsp. salt
¼ tsp. pepper
About 4 lb. boneless
  beef roast
2 medium onions,
  sliced
1 c. sliced celery
3 cooking apples,
  cored and sliced
  in wedges
2 Tbsp. cornstarch
¼ c. cold water
1 c. sliced green sweet
  peppers
  (optional)

In large food storage bag, combine first 6 ingredients; mix well. Place meat in bag and seal. Chill 12 to 24 hours, turning bag occasionally. Remove meat from bag and place in 3 quart casserole. Top with onions, celery, and peppers. Pour on marinade. Cover and roast at 325° for 2½ or 3 hours, until meat is tender. Add apples for last 10 minutes of cooking. Remove meat, vegetables, and apples. Thicken pan juices with cornstarch mixed in ¼ cup water. *Melts in your mouth!!*

APPLE MEATLOAF

1 lb. lean ground beef
1 apple, cored and
  chopped
1 medium onion,
  chopped
½ tsp. garlic salt
⅛ tsp. pepper
1 to 2 slices bread

Preheat oven to 350°. Combine all ingredients, except bread. Soak bread in cold water, squeeze out moisture, shred, and add. Place in loaf pan and bake 25 to 30 minutes. Serves 4.

BARBEQUE SALMON

¼ c. fresh apple cider
6 Tbsp. soy sauce
2 Tbsp. unsalted
butter
1 large clove garlic,
crushed through
a press
2 salmon fillets (2½ to
3 lb. each) or 4
to 5 lb. salmon
steaks, cut 1
inch thick
Sprigs of parsley or
coriander and lemon
slices for garnish

1. In a small non-corrodible saucepan, combine cider and soy sauce. Bring to a boil over high heat; reduce the heat to moderate and simmer for 3 minutes. Add the butter and garlic; continue cooking, stirring occasionally until the liquid thickens enough to coat the back of a spoon (about 20 minutes). Remove the marinade from heat and cool to room temperature.

2. Pat the salmon dry and place, skin side down, on a rack. Brush the marinade evenly over the salmon. Let stand at room temperature 30 minutes.

3. To cook outdoors: When the coals are hot, oil the rack and place, skin side down, on the grill. Tent with aluminum foil and "bake" until flesh is slightly translucent in the thickest part (about 15 to 20 minutes). Better not to turn.

4. To cook indoors: Put the salmon, skin side down, on a well oiled broiler rack and broil 6 inches from the heat until the top is glazed and flesh translucent (12 to 15 minutes). Garnish with parsley or coriander and lemon slices. Serves 8 to 10.

FAR EAST SHRIMP AND APPLES

2 cans shrimp
3 c. water
1 tsp. salt
¾ c. wild rice
¼ c. butter
½ c. chopped onions
1 c. uncooked white
  rice
½ tsp. curry powder
1 tart medium apple,
  peeled and
  chopped
2 chicken bouillon
  cubes, dissolved in 1¾
  c. boiling water
1 Tbsp. soy sauce
1 small jar sliced
  pimento

Drain and rinse shrimp. Bring water to rapid boil; add wild rice. Cover and cook for 15 minutes. Drain. Heat butter in heavy 1½ quart saucepan. Saute onion 5 minutes or until golden, stirring constantly. Add white rice and chopped apple; stir in bouillon, curry powder, soy sauce, and pimento. Add wild rice and shrimp. Cover and simmer 20 minutes over low heat, without stirring. Serves 6.

SEAFOOD APPLE CASSEROLE

6 apples, diced
$^1/_2$ c. butter
$^1/_2$ lb. shrimp
$^1/_2$ lb. scallops
2 cloves garlic, finely
  diced
$1^1/_2$ c. cooked rice
$^1/_2$ c. apple cider
Salt and pepper to
  taste
$^1/_2$ Tbsp. paprika
3 sprigs fresh parsley
  (garnish)

Saute apples over medium heat in 2 tablespoons of the butter until soft. Puree apples. Saute shrimp, scallops and garlic over medium heat in another 2 tablespoons butter for about 7 minutes. Spread rice evenly in a 9x13 inch baking pan. Spread apple puree evenly on top of rice; add apple cider. Arrange shrimp and scallops over rice; pour over them the butter used for cooking them. Add seasonings. Melt remaining $^1/_4$ cup of butter and pour over all. Bake at 350° for 30 minutes. Garnish with parsley. Yield: 4 servings.

Note: Onions may be added for additional flavor while apples are being cooked. Fillet of sole may be used instead of shrimp and scallops. Lemon slices may be used as a garnish.

ROAST LAMB WITH APPLES

3 lb. boneless sirloin
  lamb roast
$^1/_2$ lemon
2 medium to large
  apples, sliced
8 prunes, halved and
  pitted
1 Tbsp. sugar
2 to 3 cloves garlic,
  sliced
1 Tbsp. ginger
Salt and pepper to
  taste
1 Tbsp. vegetable oil
2 c. apple cider or
  juice

Rub the lamb on all sides with the juice of the lemon. Arrange apple slices and prune halves symmetrically on the meat. Sprinkle with sugar. Roll the meat up carefully and tie with string; skewer if necessary. Using a thin knife, insert garlic slices under the top skin of the meat. Rub skin with a mixture of ginger, salt, and pepper. Brush with oil until the spices adhere to the meat.

Heat apple cider or juice and use to baste the meat every 15 minutes or so. Cook for about 20 minutes to the pound to desired doneness. (Delicious when served slightly pink.) Serve with a gravy prepared from the pan juices. Slice carefully so the filling remains in the center when served. Yield: About 9 servings.

BREADS, ROLLS

APPLE BUTTER BREAD

½ c. butter or
  margarine,
  softened
1 c. brown sugar,
  firmly packed
1 egg
¾ c. buttermilk
2 tsp. soda
2 c. flour
1 c. apple butter
1 tsp. cinnamon
1 tsp. nutmeg
1 tsp. allspice
½ tsp. cloves
½ c. pecans

Cream butter and sugar. Add egg and beat well. Combine buttermilk and soda. Combine flour and spices. Add alternately with buttermilk, beginning and ending with flour. Stir in apple butter and pecans. Pour into greased and floured 9x5x3 inch loaf pan. Bake at 350° for 1 hour or until wooden pick inserted comes out clean. Cool in pan for 5 minutes; remove to wire rack and cool completely. Makes 1 loaf. *Makes nice gift.*

CHEDDAR APPLE BREAD

½ c. shortening
½ c. sugar
1 egg
1 (20 oz.) can apple
  pie filling
2½ c. sifted flour
1 tsp. salt
1 tsp. baking soda
1 tsp. baking powder
1 c. shredded Cheddar
  cheese
½ c. chopped walnuts

Cream shortening and sugar. Add egg. Beat in apple pie filling. Sift the flour, salt, soda, and baking powder together and add to creamed mixture. Add the cheese and walnuts. Pour into well greased loaf pan. Bake at 350° for 1½ hours. Makes 16 to 20 servings.

FRESH APPLE BREAD

1 c. sugar
2 eggs, beaten
½ tsp. salt
1 c. chopped pecans
½ tsp. vanilla
1 tsp. cinnamon
½ c. shortening
1 c. grated apple
1 tsp. soda
1½ Tbsp. buttermilk
3 Tbsp. sugar and cinnamon (for top)
2 c. flour

Cream butter and sugar. Add egg and apple. Mix in sifted dry ingredients to which nuts have been added. Stir in milk and vanilla. Pour into greased and floured pans. Sprinkle top with cinnamon and sugar. Bake at 350° for 1 hour.

APPLESAUCE NUT BREAD

2 c. flour, sifted
¾ c. sugar
2 tsp. baking powder
1 tsp. salt
½ tsp. baking soda
½ tsp. cinnamon
1 c. nutmeats
1 egg, beaten
1 c. thick applesauce
2 Tbsp. shortening, melted

Sift flour, baking powder, salt, soda, and cinnamon together. Add nutmeats, beaten egg, applesauce, and slightly cooled shortening to sifted dry ingredients. Stir until blended. Pour into greased loaf bread pan. Bake 1 hour in 350° oven or until done to the touch.

APPLE-BANANA BREAD

1 c. shortening
¾ c. sugar
3 Tbsp. buttermilk
2 eggs, well beaten
1 banana, mashed
1 c. applesauce
2 c. flour (plain)
1 tsp. soda
1 tsp. salt

Mix shortening and sugar and beat for 2 minutes. Add buttermilk and eggs; beat well. Sift dry ingredients together and slowly add to first mixture. Thoroughly blend. Pour into greased loaf pan. Bake at 350° for 45 minutes.

The bread freezes well.

CREAMY APPLE ALMOND CRUNCH BREAD

Filling:
2 (3 oz.) pkg. cream
   cheese
2 Tbsp. sugar
1 egg
½ c. chopped, peeled
   apple

Bread:
1 pkg. apple
   cinnamon quick
   bread
½ c. chopped, peeled
   apples
¾ c. water
3 Tbsp. oil
1 egg
1 tsp. almond extract

Topping:
¼ c. sliced almonds
Apple jelly

Preheat oven. Grease and flour 8x4 or 9x5 inch loaf pan. In small bowl, blend all filling ingredients, except apple. Beat at medium speed until smooth. Stir in apples. Set aside.

In large bowl, combine all bread ingredients. Stir by hand until mix is moistened. Pour half of batter into pan. Carefully spoon cream cheese filling over batter. Spoon remaining batter on top of filling. Sprinkle with almonds. Bake for 70 to 85 minutes for 8x4 inch pan and 65 to 75 minutes for 9x5 inch pan or until toothpick inserted near center comes out clean. Cool 15 minutes. Remove from pan. Cool completely. Brush with melted apple jelly. Store in refrigerator.

APPLE CORN BREAD

½ c. sugar
2 c. flour
2 eggs
1 c. corn meal
⅔ c. oil
1 tsp. baking powder
Milk
1 can apple filling
1 Tbsp. sugar
1 tsp. cinnamon

Mix together the sugar, flour, eggs, corn meal, oil, baking powder, and enough milk to make it like a cake batter. Pour into a greased and floured pan. Take 1 can apple filling with 1 tablespoon and 1 teaspoon cinnamon. Pour over top of batter. Bake at 350° for 25 to 30 minutes in a 9x13 inch pan until done. Yields 8 servings.

You may use another type fruit filling and omit the cinnamon.

UPSIDE-DOWN APPLE GINGERBREAD

A spicy gingerbread topped with caramel apple slices.

½ c. melted butter
½ c. molasses
½ c. white sugar
1 egg
2 c. all-purpose flour
1 tsp. ginger
1 tsp. cinnamon
½ tsp. ground cloves
¼ tsp. nutmeg
½ tsp. salt
1 tsp. baking soda
¾ c. plus 2 Tbsp. hot
   tea or water

Apple layer:
3 Tbsp. melted butter
⅓ c. brown sugar
3 apples

Combine butter, molasses, sugar, and egg in a large mixing bowl and beat until well-mixed. Sift flour, ginger, cinnamon, cloves, nutmeg, and salt into a medium bowl. Stir into butter mixture and mix well. Dissolve baking soda in hot tea or water and add to batter. Mix well. Pour melted butter into a 9 inch square baking pan. Sprinkle evenly with brown sugar. Peel, quarter, core, and slice apples. Spread apple slices evenly in pan. Pour batter over apples. Bake at 350° for 35 to 40 minutes or until a cake tester comes out clean. Invert onto a plate. Serve warm with ice cream or whipped cream. Serves 9.

FRESH APPLE GINGERBREAD

½ c. margarine
½ c. sugar
2 eggs
⅔ c. molasses
2 c. flour
1½ tsp. baking soda
¾ tsp. salt
½ tsp. cinnamon and
  nutmeg
¼ tsp. cloves
⅓ c. milk
1¼ c. grated, pared
  apple (1 large
  apple)

Cream together butter and sugar. Beat in eggs, one at a time. Blend in molasses. Mix flour, baking soda, salt, ginger, cinnamon, nutmeg, and cloves; add to creamed mixture alternately with milk, beginning and ending with flour mixture. Stir in grated apple. Pour into greased and floured 9x9x2 inch baking pan. Bake in 350° oven 45 to 50 minutes or until cake tester inserted in center comes out clean. Cool in pan 10 minutes; turn out onto rack. Serve warm. Yield: 9 to 12 servings.

INDIAN PUMPKIN-APPLESAUCE BREAD

⅔ c. butter or
  shortening
4 c. brown sugar
1 c. crushed pumpkin,
  cooked
4 eggs
3½ c. flour
1 c. apple juice
½ tsp. nutmeg
1 c. nuts, chopped
  (walnuts or pecans)
1½ tsp. cinnamon
½ tsp. baking powder
2 Tbsp. baking soda
1 c. applesauce

Cream butter and sugar together, then add the eggs, one a a time, beating all together real well. Stir in applesauce and pumpkin. Now sift the dry ingredients together and add with the apple juice. Now stir in nuts and pour into 2 greased bread loaf pans. Bake for 1 hour in a 350° oven.

41

ZUCCHINI APPLE BREAD

3 small eggs, beaten
¾ c. sugar
¾ c. oil
1½ c. flour
1 tsp. salt (optional)
1 tsp. cinnamon
1 tsp. nutmeg
1 grated apple
1½ c. grated zucchini
1 tsp. vanilla

Heat oven to 350°. Grease bottom of loaf pan. Beat eggs and add sugar. Beat until creamy. Add oil. Add dry ingredients. Mix well. Add apples, zucchini, and vanilla; mix well. Pour into pan. Bake until toothpick comes out clean, about 55 minutes. Cool 10 minutes in pan. Remove and slice warm; spread with butter if desired.

APPLE STREUSEL LADDER LOAF

16 oz. loaf frozen
   sweet bread
   dough or bread
   dough, thawed
2 Tbsp. butter or
   margarine,
   softened
¼ c. packed brown
   sugar
1 Tbsp. flour
1 tsp. cinnamon
2 c. finely chopped,
   peeled apples (use a tart
   apple)
Milk
2 Tbsp. flour
2 Tbsp. sugar
1 Tbsp. butter or
   margarine
¼ c. slivered almonds
   (optional)

Divide thawed dough in half. On a lightly floured surface, roll each half into an 8 inch square. Spread each square with 1 tablespoon butter. In a bowl, combine brown sugar, 1 tablespoon flour, and cinnamon; add apples and mix to coat. Spread half of the filling down the center of each square. Cutting from the right edge toward the filling, make 2½ inch long cuts in dough at 1 inch intervals. Repeat from the left edge. Fold strips alternately over filling, folding under edges. Place braided loaves on greased jellyroll pan. Brush with milk. Combine the 2 tablespoons flour and sugar. Cut in 1 tablespoon butter. Sprinkle this mixture over loaves and top with nuts. Bake in 350° oven until brown and apples pierce easily.

TINY RAISIN APPLE LOAVES

⅓ c. butter or
   margarine,
   softened
⅔ c. sugar
2 eggs
1 tsp. lemon juice
3 Tbsp. milk
2 c. sifted flour
1 tsp. salt
½ tsp. baking soda
1 c. grated raw apple
1 c. chopped raisins

Cream together butter, sugar, and eggs until light and fluffy. Beat in milk and lemon juice. Sift together dry ingredients; stir into creamed mixture just until moistened. Stir in apples and raisins. Bake at 350° for 40 to 45 minutes or until toothpick inserted in center comes out clean.

GLAZED APPLE LOAF

1 stick margarine
1 c. sugar
2 Tbsp. milk
2 c. flour
½ tsp. salt
1 tsp. vanilla
2 eggs
1 c. finely chopped
   apples
2½ tsp. baking
   powder
1 tsp. cinnamon

Apple Loaf Glaze:
½ c. powdered sugar
2 Tbsp. softened
   margarine
1 Tbsp. water
½ tsp. cinnamon

Cream together margarine, vanilla, and sugar until fluffy. Add eggs, one at a time. Add milk and apples. Blend together flour, baking powder, salt, and cinnamon. Mix well and place in a 9x5 inch sprayed loaf pan. Bake 1 hour at 350°. Cool and glaze.

Glaze: Mix glaze ingredients and drizzle over loaf.

43

APPLE COFFEECAKE

1 egg, beaten
½ c. granulated sugar
½ c. milk
2 Tbsp. melted butter
1 c. flour
2 tsp. baking powder
½ tsp. salt (optional)

Topping:
¼ to ½ c. brown sugar
1 tsp. cinnamon
1 Tbsp. flour
1 Tbsp. butter
1 apple, sliced
2 tsp. broken walnuts

Grease a 9 inch round cake pan liberally, using butter. Beat the egg until frothy, then stir in the sugar, milk, and melted butter. Mix the dry ingredients together, then stir them into the batter. Pour the batter into cake pan.

For the topping, mix together the brown sugar, flour, and cinnamon. Cut in the butter. If desired, stir in nuts. Dust this mixture over the top of the batter, then poke thin slices of apple through the topping and into the batter. Bake at 375° for 25 to 30 minutes.

Note: This may be baked at once, refrigerated overnight, or even frozen before baking.

APPLE COFFEECAKE

1 yellow cake mix
3 eggs
1 can apple pie filling

Topping:
1 stick oleo
½ c. confectioners
 sugar
1 c. flour

Mix together and divide into 2 (9x5 inch) greased pans (bread). Mix together with pastry blender. Place on top of first mixture and bake in 350° oven for 50 minutes.

APPLE DANISH

Danish:
1 c. shortening
3 c. flour
½ tsp. salt
1 egg, separated
½ c. milk
6 c. apple slices
½ c. butter or
   margarine
1 tsp. cinnamon
1½ c. sugar
2 Tbsp. flour

Glaze:
¾ c. confectioners
   sugar
⅛ tsp. salt
1 to 2 Tbsp. milk

Cream shortening into flour. Combine egg yolks and milk and add to flour mixture. Roll out ½ dough and pat in jellyroll pan (11 x 16 x ½ inch). Arrange apple slices on crust. Mix sugar, cinnamon, and flour and sprinkle on the apple slices. Dot with butter. Roll out rest of dough and cover apples. Brush with slightly beaten egg white. Bake at 375° for 45 minutes. Top with glaze mixture while still warm. Makes 20 servings.

APPLE STRUDEL PUFF

2 Tbsp. butter or
  margarine
3 eggs
¾ c. sifted flour
¾ c. milk
1 (20 oz.) can apple
  pie filling
¼ c. light brown sugar

Preheat oven to 500°. Place butter in 10 inch skillet with ovenproof handle; set in oven to melt butter while oven heats.

Combine eggs, flour, and milk in a medium size bowl; beat until smooth. Remove skillet from oven and tip to coat side with butter; pour in batter. Place in oven; turn temperature to 425°. Bake 20 minutes, or until puffed and golden. While puff bakes, place apples in a medium size saucepan and heat until bubbly. Spoon into puff as soon as it comes from the oven; sprinkle brown sugar on top. Cut puff into wedges. Place on serving plates and serve hot. Serves 4.

Note: Batter puffs into all kinds of fascinating shapes as it bakes and each recipe you make may look different. If your oven does not have a glass door, do not be tempted to peek until baking is finished.

APPLE-CINNAMON PULL APARTS

1 (16 oz.) frozen bread
  dough
Apple pastry pie filling
3 Tbsp. butter
⅓ c. sugar
Cinnamon (add to
  sugar to taste)

Cut dough in half lengthwise, then cut into 8 pieces crosswise. Flatten and stretch to form 4 inch circles. Spoon 1 tablespoon pie filling into each circle. Bring edges of dough together and pinch to seal. Dip in melted butter, then in cinnamon sugar. Place, seam down, in 2 layers in a 9x5x3 inch loaf pan and let rise until double. Bake at 350° for 35 to 40 minutes with foil for last 10 minutes. Remove from oven and invert on plate.

EASY APPLE DOUGHNUTS

2 c. all-purpose flour
¼ c. sugar
3 tsp. baking powder
½ tsp. salt
½ tsp. cinnamon
½ tsp. nutmeg
½ c. half & half
⅓ c. frozen apple juice
  concentrate,
  thawed
1 egg, slightly beaten
Oil for deep-frying
⅓ c. sugar
½ tsp. cinnamon

Mix first 6 ingredients and blend well. Add half & half, apple juice concentrate, and egg; stir thoroughly with fork. In 3 quart saucepan, heat 3 to 4 inches oil to approximately 375°. Drop by teaspoonful into hot oil, 5 or 6 at a time. Fry until golden brown, 1 to 1½ minutes each side. Drain on paper towels. Roll warm doughnuts in the ⅓ cup sugar and ½ teaspoon cinnamon. Makes 30 to 35 doughnut balls.

APPLE FRITTERS

1 egg, beaten
1 c. milk
1 c. finely chopped,
  unpeeled, cored apple
¼ c. sugar
¼ tsp. salt
1 tsp. orange peel,
  grated
3 Tbsp. orange juice
1 tsp. orange peel
1 tsp. vanilla
2 c. flour
1 Tbsp. baking
  powder
Fat for frying
Sifted confectioners
  sugar

Mix all ingredients together, except flour and baking powder. Stir together flour and baking powder; fold into egg mixture, stirring just until all of the flour is moist. Drop batter by rounded teaspoons into deep hot fat (350°). Fry until deep golden brown, about 3 minutes, turning once. Drain on paper towels, then roll in confectioners sugar. Serve warm.

47

BAKED APPLE PANCAKE

1 large tart apple,
   peeled and
   sliced
Butter
½ c. milk
½ c. all-purpose flour
1 tsp. sugar
Dash of salt
3 eggs
Ground cinnamon
Confectioners sugar
Lemon juice

Preheat oven to 500°. Fry apple slices in small amount of butter until softened, but not mushy. Place apple slices in 8 or 9 inch pie pan or other baking dishes. Thoroughly mix milk, flour, salt, dash of cinnamon, and eggs in blender or with mixer. Pour batter over apples. Bake in oven 7 to 8 minutes. Pancake will puff up. Remove from oven and dot with more butter. Sprinkle with cinnamon, confectioners sugar, and lemon juice. Makes 2 to 4 servings.

APPLE PANCAKES

2 eggs
2 c. buttermilk
¼ c. oil
1¾ c. flour
2 Tbsp. sugar
2 tsp. baking powder
1 tsp. baking soda
½ tsp. salt
1 c. peeled apple,
   shredded
½ tsp. cinnamon

Beat eggs; stir in buttermilk and oil. Add flour and remaining ingredients; stir just until large lumps disappear. Heat griddle to medium-high and lightly grease. Pour batter onto hot griddle and bake until done. Serves 16.

APPLE BUTTER MUFFINS

1¾ c. all-purpose
   flour
⅓ c. sugar
2 tsp. baking powder
1 tsp. apple pie spice*
   or pumpkin pie
   spice
¼ tsp. salt
1 egg, beaten
¾ c. milk
¼ c. cooking oil
⅓ c. apple butter
⅓ c. pecans, chopped
2 Tbsp. sugar

In a medium mixing bowl, combine the flour, sugar, baking powder, pie spice, and salt. Make a well in the center. Combine the egg, milk, and oil; add all at once to flour mixture. Stir just until moistened. Lightly grease muffin cups or line with paper baking cups. Spoon a rounded tablespoon of batter into each muffin cup. Top each with a rounded teaspoon of apple butter and then with the remaining batter. Combine pecans and the 2 tablespoons sugar; sprinkle on top of batter. Bake in a 400° oven for about 20 minutes or until golden. Serve warm. Makes 12 muffins.

If frozen, to defrost, place 2 muffins on a paper towel and microwave on HIGH (100%) for 50 to 60 seconds.

* Apple pie spice: One-half teaspoon cinnamon, ¼ teaspoon nutmeg, ⅛ teaspoon allspice, and a dash of ginger.

FRESH APPLE SPICE MUFFINS

¾ c. milk
2 eggs, beaten
¼ c. melted margarine
2 c. unsifted flour
½ c. sugar
1 Tbsp. baking
   powder
½ tsp. salt
1 tsp. cinnamon
1 c. finely chopped
   apples (about 2)
¼ c. raisins

Add milk to eggs; stir in margarine. Mix dry ingredients thoroughly; stir in apples and raisins. Add liquid mixture and stir just until most of the dry ingredients are moistened. Do not overmix. Batter should be lumpy. Fill greased muffin tins ⅔ full. Bake at 400° (hot oven) for 20 to 25 minutes until golden brown. Makes 12 muffins.

CINNAMON-APPLESAUCE MUFFINS

¼ c. sugar
½ tsp. ground
  cinnamon
2 c. baking mix
¾ c. unsweetened
  applesauce
⅓ c. chopped nuts (if
  desired)
3 Tbsp. vegetable oil
½ tsp. ground
  cinnamon
¼ tsp. ground nutmeg
¼ tsp. ground allspice
1 egg
3 Tbsp. margarine or
  butter, melted

Preheat oven to 450°. Line 12 medium muffin cups with paper baking cups. Mix granulated sugar and ½ teaspoon cinnamon; reserve. Mix remaining ingredients, except margarine, with fork until moistened. Divide batter among muffin cups. Bake until golden brown, 15 to 20 minutes. Immediately remove from muffin cups. While warm, dip tops with melted margarine, then into sugar-cinnamon mixture. Makes 12 muffins.

50

APPLE MUFFINS

1 can apple pie filling
1 c. sugar
½ c. oil
2 eggs
1 tsp. vanilla
2 c. flour
1 tsp. cinnamon
1 tsp. baking powder
1 tsp. baking soda
½ tsp. salt
Walnuts or raisins
(optional)

Topping:
½ c. brown sugar
3 Tbsp. white sugar
¼ c. margarine
3 Tbsp. flour
1 tsp. cinnamon
½ c. nuts

For muffins: Mix sugars, oil, eggs, and vanilla. Add pie filling, then dry ingredients. Fill muffin tins ½ full. Sprinkle topping over batter. Bake at 350° for 15 to 20 minutes.

OATMEAL APPLE RAISIN MUFFINS

1 egg
¾ c. milk
1 c. raisins
1 chopped apple
½ c. oil
2 tsp. cinnamon
1 c. all-purpose flour
1 c. quick oats
⅓ c. sugar
3 tsp. baking powder
1 tsp. salt
1 tsp. nutmeg

Beat egg; stir in remaining ingredients, mixing just to moisten. Pour in 12 greased muffin cups until ¾ full. Bake at 400° for 15 to 20 minutes. Serve cool or piping hot with butter.

51

CHEESY BACON 'N APPLE MUFFINS

2 c. sifted all-purpose
   flour
¼ c. sugar
4 tsp. baking powder
¾ tsp. salt
1 c. milk
⅓ c. butter, melted
1 egg, slightly beaten
½ c. finely chopped,
   unpeeled apple
¾ c. (3 oz.) shredded
   aged Cheddar
   cheese
⅔ c. crisp bacon,
   crumbled (about
   8 slices)

In large bowl, sift together flour, sugar, baking powder, and salt. In small bowl, combine milk, butter, and egg; stir into dry ingredients just until moistened. Fold in apple, cheese, and bacon crumbles. Spoon into buttered muffin cups, filling ⅔ full. Bake in preheated 400° oven 15 to 20 minutes or until golden brown. Remove from pan. Cool on wire rack. Makes 18 muffins.

DESSERTS

DOWN EAST APPLE PIE

Crust:
2½ c. flour
½ tsp. salt
1 c. shortening
8 to 10 Tbsp. ice water

Apple Filling:
8 to 10 Cortland
   apples
⅓ c. flour
1 tsp. cinnamon
¾ tsp. nutmeg
Pinch of salt
5 to 6 pats butter

Cranberry Base:
2 c. cranberries
1 c. sugar
½ c. orange juice
½ c. water
Zest from 1 orange
Dash of nutmeg

Heat oven to 400°. Prepare crust in classic tradition. Cut shortening into flour and salt; add tablespoons of ice water to mixture and stir in gently and quickly. Feel often with fingers until mix is moist and will stick together. Chill about 1 hour in damp cloth.

Cook cranberry base over low heat and reduce by ⅓ (approximately 1¾ cups). Cool. Peel apples and cut into thin slices. Mix dry ingredients and pour over apples. Gently toss apples in large mixing bowl until all slices are covered. Roll out bottom half (½ of crust) and place into 10 inch glass pie plate. Pour 1¾ cups of cranberry base on crust and top with apple mixture. Top with pats of butter. Place top crust on apples. Be sure to wet edge of bottom crust with water so that seal will be firm. Press edges gently but firmly and trim excess crust. Fold crust into edge of pie plate and form edge to your design. Moisten top with milk and sprinkle with sugar. Cut slits in pie top and bake. Cook 50 minutes. When baking 2 pies, change position of pies in oven.

 53

FRESH APPLE PIE

9 inch pie crust
¾ c. sugar
¼ c. all-purpose flour
½ tsp. ground nutmeg
½ tsp. ground
  cinnamon
Dash of salt
6 c. thinly sliced,
  pared apple
2 Tbsp. margarine or
  butter

Heat oven to 425°. Prepare pastry. Mix sugar, flour, nutmeg, cinnamon, and salt. Stir in apples. Turn into pastry lined pie plate; dot with margarine. Cover with top crust that has slits cut in it; seal and flute. Cover edge with 3 inch strip of aluminum foil. Bake until crust is brown and juice begins to bubble through slits of crust, 40 to 50 minutes.

SOUR CREAM APPLE PIE

2 eggs
1 c. sour cream (8 oz.)
1 c. sugar
6 Tbsp. flour, divided
1 tsp. vanilla
¼ tsp. salt
3 c. chopped, peeled
  apples
1 (9 inch) unbaked pie
  shell
3 Tbsp. melted butter
  or oleo
¼ c. packed brown
  sugar

In large bowl, beat eggs. Add sour cream. Stir in sugar, 2 tablespoons flour, vanilla, and salt. Mix well. Stir in apples. Pour into pie shell. Bake at 375° for 15 minutes.

Meanwhile, combine butter, brown sugar, and remaining flour. Sprinkle over top of pie. Return to oven for 20 to 25 minutes or until filling is set. Cool completely on wire rack. Serve or cover and refrigerate. Yields 8 servings.

BUTTER CRUST APPLE CHERRY PIE

2½ c. flour
1 tsp. salt
¾ c. shortening
⅓ c. cold water
4 tart apples
6 Tbsp. butter
1 c. sugar
1 (No. 2) can pitted
  sour cherries
2 Tbsp. flour
1 tsp. cinnamon
½ tsp. nutmeg

Mix first 4 ingredients to make pie crust. Line 9 inch pie plate with dough. Pare, core, and slice apples. Melt 2 tablespoons butter and brush on bottom of crust. Arrange apples in pie shell. Drain cherries and place on top of apples.

Mix sugar, flour, cinnamon, and nutmeg. Sprinkle on fruit. Dot with 2 tablespoons butter and cover with pastry. Bake at 425° for 30 to 40 minutes. Melt remaining butter and brush on top of crust. Bake for 10 more minutes.

PEAR AND APPLE PIE

3 c. pears, pared and
  thinly sliced
3 c. apples, pared and
  thinly sliced
¾ c. sugar
3 Tbsp. flour
½ tsp. cinnamon
¼ tsp. salt
1 (9 inch) unbaked pie
  shell

Topping:
⅓ c. margarine
½ c. brown sugar
1 c. flour

Combine pears, apples, sugar, flour, cinnamon, and salt. Place in unbaked pie shell.

Topping: Cream margarine and brown sugar. Mix in flour. Sprinkle over top of pie.

Fold a 14 inch circle of foil loosely over top and around sides of pie. Bake at 400° for 40 to 45 minutes. Remove foil and continue baking for 20 minutes longer.

APPLE MACAROON PIE

1 unbaked pastry shell
4 c. thinly sliced
  apples
½ c. sugar
1 Tbsp. flour
½ tsp. cinnamon
½ tsp. salt
2 tsp. butter

Coconut Topping:
1 well beaten egg
½ c. sugar
1 c. shredded coconut
¼ c. milk

Line 9 inch pie pan with pastry and arrange apple slices in pan. Combine sugar with flour, cinnamon, and salt. Sprinkle mixture on top of apples. Dot with butter and bake in 425° oven for 20 minutes. Add Coconut Topping; lower heat to 350° and bake for 30 minutes longer. Serves 8.

Coconut Topping: Combine well beaten egg, sugar, shredded coconut, and milk. Spread over top of partially baked pie.

CRUNCHY APPLESAUCE PIE

1 can applesauce
½ c. sugar
1 tsp. cinnamon
1½ tsp. lemon juice
1 egg
½ c. evaporated milk
¼ tsp. salt
½ c. sugar
2 c. coconut

Mix applesauce, ½ cup sugar, cinnamon, and lemon juice. Pour into pie shell and bake for 20 minutes.

Meanwhile, mix egg, evaporated milk, salt, ½ cup sugar, and coconut. Remove pie from oven and spoon mixture over top. Return to oven and reduce heat to 375°. Bake until brown.

AUTUMN CHEESECAKE

Crust:
1 c. graham cracker
  crust
3 Tbsp. sugar
½ tsp. cinnamon
¼ c. margarine,
  melted

Filling:
2 (8 oz.) pkg. cream
  cheese, softened
½ c. sugar
2 eggs
½ tsp. vanilla

Topping:
4 c. thin peeled apple
  slices
½ tsp. cinnamon
⅓ c. sugar
¼ c. chopped pecans

Combine crumbs, sugar, cinnamon, and margarine. Press into bottom of 9 inch springform pan. Bake at 350° for 10 minutes or freeze to set. Combine cream cheese and sugar, mixing at medium speed on electric mixer until well blended. Add eggs, one at a time, mixing well after each addition. Blend in vanilla; pour over crust. Toss apples with combined sugar and cinnamon. Spoon apple mixture over cream cheese layer. Sprinkle with pecans. Bake at 350° for 1 hour and 10 minutes. Loosen cake from rim of pan; cool before removing rim of pan. Chill.

FRESH APPLE CAKE

2 c. sugar
3 eggs
1½ c. oil
3 c. plain flour
½ tsp. salt
1 tsp. baking soda
2 tsp. vanilla
1 c. nuts
2 to 3 c. diced apples
1 c. raisins (optional)

Topping:
1 stick margarine
½ c. brown sugar
2 Tbsp. evaporated
   milk

Mix together sugar, oil, vanilla, and eggs. Beat for 3 minutes. Add soda and salt to plain flour and mix together. Add eggs and nuts. Bake for 1 to 1¼ hours at 325°.

Topping: Mix margarine, brown sugar, and evaporated milk together. Pour over warm cake after punching top of cake with a fork so topping can drain into cake. Add Cool Whip when serving (optional).

QUICK APPLE CAKE

1¾ c. sugar
1 c. salad oil
3 eggs
2 c. flour
1 tsp. baking soda
1 tsp. vanilla
½ tsp. salt
4 medium apples,
   peeled and chopped
¾ c. walnuts, chopped
1 tsp. cinnamon

Cream Cheese
   Frosting:
1 (6 oz.) pkg. cream
   cheese
¾ stick margarine
1 Tbsp. milk
3 c. powdered sugar

Mix all ingredients, except apples, mixing well. Fold in apples. Batter will be thick. Pour in oiled and floured 9x13 inch baking pan. Bake at 350° for 45 minutes. Frost with Cream Cheese Frosting.

Cream Cheese Frosting: Mix well. Spread over cooled cake.

This cake is best when made the night before serving.

59

APPLE BLOSSOM BUNDT CAKE

A great "coffee" cake - good anytime!

1½ c. vegetable oil
2 c. sugar
3 eggs
3 c. flour
1½ tsp. soda
1 tsp. salt
½ tsp. cinnamon
½ tsp. ground cloves
½ tsp. nutmeg
1 tsp. vanilla
3 c. apples (unpeeled),
  chopped
  (Jonathan apples
  preferred)
½ c. English walnuts
  or pecans,
  chopped

Heat oven to 325°. Cream oil and sugar together. Add eggs, one at a time, beating well. Sift dry ingredients and spices together. Add to sugar mixture. Add vanilla, apples, and nuts to batter; fold all together. Bake in a well greased Bundt pan for 1 hour and 15 minutes. Cool for 20 minutes before removing from pan. Serve warm or cool without icing.

APPLE BLACK WALNUT CAKE

4 c. raw apples,
  chopped
  coarsely
2 c. sugar
3 eggs
¾ c. oil
2 tsp. vanilla
2 c. sifted all-purpose
  flour
2 tsp. baking soda
1 tsp. cinnamon
½ tsp. nutmeg
1 c. chopped black
  walnuts
1 tsp. salt

Lemon Butter
  Frosting:
3 c. confectioners
  sugar
4 Tbsp. butter
2 Tbsp. lemon juice
1 or 2 Tbsp. cold water
1 tsp. lemon extract
Dash of salt

Combine apples and sugar; let stand. Beat eggs slightly; beat in oil and vanilla. Sift together flour, salt, soda, and spices. Stir in, alternating ingredients; add walnuts. Pour into a greased and floured 9x13 inch pan. Bake at 350° for about an hour or until done. Cool, then cover with Lemon Butter Frosting.

Lemon Butter Frosting: Mix well and frost.

APPLESAUCE CAKE

2 c. applesauce
1½ c. sugar
1 c. shortening
2 eggs
3 c. flour
1½ tsp. cloves
1½ tsp. cinnamon
1½ tsp. soda
½ tsp. salt
2 c. raisins
2 c. nuts

Cream sugar, shortening, and 2 eggs; add applesauce and beat together. Add flour, soda, salt, and spices that have been sifted together. Fold in raisins and nuts. Bake in an angel food cake pan for 1 hour at 350°.

APPLESAUCE-OATMEAL CAKE

1¼ c. sweetened
    applesauce
¾ c. quick cooking
    rolled oats
1 c. raisins (optional)
½ c. shortening
¾ c. brown sugar
1 egg
1 tsp. vanilla
1½ c. sifted all-
    purpose flour
1 tsp. baking powder
½ tsp. soda
½ tsp. salt
½ tsp. cinnamon
¼ c. chopped nuts
2 Tbsp. sugar

Heat applesauce to boiling; stir in rolled oats and raisins. Cool. Cream shortening and brown sugar until light and fluffy; add egg and vanilla, beating thoroughly. Sift flour with baking powder, soda, salt, and cinnamon. Add to creamed mixture alternately with applesauce, beating until smooth after each addition. Stir in nuts. Turn into greased and floured 9x9x2 inch pan. Spread sugar lightly over cake. Bake at 350° for 50 minutes or until done. Makes 12 servings.

DUTCH APPLE CAKE

Crust:
1¼ c. flour
¾ tsp. baking powder
½ tsp. salt
1 tsp. sugar
½ c. butter
1 egg yolk, beaten
2 Tbsp. milk

Topping:
3 to 4 c. peeled,
   chopped or
   sliced apples
¾ c. sugar
1½ Tbsp. flour
½ tsp. cinnamon
3 Tbsp. butter

To make crust, sift flour with baking powder, salt, and sugar. Cut the butter into the flour mixture; moisten with the egg and milk mixture. Press into bottom of 11x7 inch pan.

Press prepared apples over the dough of the crust. Sprinkle with topping ingredients which have been mixed like coarse crumbs. Bake at 375° for 50 minutes or until apples are done.

APPLE BUTTER COOKIES

¼ c. butter, softened
1 c. packed brown
   sugar
1 egg
½ c. quick cooking
   oats
½ c. apple butter
1 c. all-purpose flour
½ tsp. baking soda
½ tsp. baking powder
½ tsp. salt
2 Tbsp. milk
½ c. nuts, chopped
½ c. raisins

In a mixing bowl, cream butter and sugar. Beat in eggs, oats, and apple butter. Combine dry ingredients; gradually add to creamed mixture along with the milk. Beat until blended. Stir in nuts and raisins. Chill well. Drop by teaspoonfuls onto lightly greased cookie sheets. Bake at 350° for 15 minutes. Makes about 2½ dozen.

APPLESAUCE-OATMEAL COOKIES

¾ c. packed brown
   sugar
½ c. butter or
   margarine
1 egg
1 c. unsweetened
   applesauce
3 c. rolled oats
1 c. flour
½ c. raisins
1¼ tsp. salt
½ tsp. baking powder
½ tsp. baking soda
½ tsp. cinnamon

Cream brown sugar and butter until light and fluffy; beat in egg, then applesauce (mixture will look curdled). Stir in oats, raisins, salt, baking powder, baking soda, and cinnamon. Drop by teaspoonfuls on greased cookie sheet. Bake in a preheated 375° oven 12 to 15 minutes or until lightly browned. Makes about 36.

APPLESAUCE MOLASSES COOKIES

2 c. brown sugar,
   packed
1 c. white sugar
½ c. lard
1 c. margarine or
   butter
1 c. molasses
3 eggs
2 tsp. pumpkin pie
   spice
1 tsp. cinnamon
1 Tbsp. vanilla
2 c. oatmeal
3 tsp. baking powder
3 tsp. baking soda
1 c. raisins
1 c. nuts
1½ c. applesauce
6 c. flour (may need a
   little more)

Mix together all ingredients and chill over-night. Roll in ball and roll in sugar. Put on cookie sheet. Bake at 350° for 10 minutes. Makes about 8 dozen large size cookies.

APPLE-FILLED OATMEAL COOKIES

1 c. peeled, chopped
  apple
½ c. sugar
¼ c. raisins
¼ c. chopped walnuts
2 Tbsp. water
1 c. butter or
  margarine,
  softened
¾ c. firmly packed
  light brown
  sugar
¼ c. sugar
1 egg
1 tsp. vanilla extract
1¼ c. all-purpose
  flour
1 tsp. salt
3 c. regular oats
  (uncooked)
1 c. flaked coconut

Combine first 5 ingredients in a medium saucepan; cook over medium heat, stirring constantly, until apple is tender and mixture thickens, about 10 minutes. Set aside.

Cream butter; gradually add brown sugar and ½ cup sugar, beating at medium speed of an electric mixer. Add egg and vanilla; mix well. Combine flour and salt; add to creamed mixture. Stir in oats and coconut; mix well. Set aside ⅓ of dough. Shape remaining dough into 48 (1 inch) balls. Place balls about 2 inches apart on ungreased cookie sheets. Press thumb in each ball of dough, leaving an indentation. Fill indentation with ½ teaspoon of apple mixture.

Shape reserved cookie dough into 48 (½ inch) balls. Flatten cookie dough in palm of hand and place on top of filling, gently pressing to seal filling in cookie. Bake at 375° for 10 to 12 minutes or until lightly browned. Remove cookies to wire racks to cool. Yield: 4 dozen.

APPLE RAISIN BARS

Crumb Mixture:
2 c. all-purpose flour
2 c. quick cooking oats
1½ c. sugar
1¼ c. sweet cream
   butter
1 tsp. baking soda

Filling:
½ c. raisins
½ c. chopped pecans
1 (20 oz.) can apple
   filling
½ tsp. cinnamon
½ tsp. nutmeg

In 3 quart bowl, combine all crumb mixture ingredients. Stir until well mixed. Reserve 1½ cups crumb mixture; set aside. Press remaining crumb mixture into ungreased 13x9 inch pan. Bake at 350° for 15 to 20 minutes.

Meanwhile, combine all filling ingredients and stir well. Spread over hot crust; sprinkle with reserved crumb mixture. Return to oven for 25 to 30 minutes. Cool completely and cut into bars. Makes 3 dozen.

FROSTED APPLE BARS

2½ c. flour
1 tsp. salt
1 c. margarine
1 egg
⅔ c. milk (scant)
1 c. corn flakes
4 large (raw) apples
1 c. sugar
1 tsp. cinnamon

Icing:
1 c. powdered sugar
1 Tbsp. hot water
1 tsp. vanilla ·

Mix flour, salt, and margarine until crumbly. Beat egg; add milk to make ⅔ cup. Mix well with preceding. Divide dough in half; roll out into pan, 9x13 inches. Sprinkle with corn flakes. Peel and slice apples and arrange on dough. Sprinkle cinnamon and sugar over apples. Roll other half of dough and put on top. Bake 1 hour at 350°. Ice while hot.

GRANDMA'S APPLE DUMPLINGS

6 tart apples, pared
and cored
1 recipe pie pastry
(recipe follows)
1 c. brown sugar
2 Tbsp. flour
½ tsp. salt
Dash of nutmeg
2 c. boiling water
½ c. butter or
margarine
Raisins and chopped
nuts (optional
for filling apple
cores)

Pie Pastry:
2 c. flour
1 tsp. salt
⅔ c. shortening
¼ c. water

Roll pastry thin and cut into 6 inch squares. Place apples in center of square and sprinkle with sugar, nutmeg, and cinnamon. Dampen edges of dough and bring opposite corners together over apples.

Make syrup by blending sugar, flour, salt, and nutmeg and add boiling water and butter. Bring to a boil and pour over dumplings. Bake, covered, at 425° for ½ hour. Uncover and bake until apples are tender and dumplings browned.

Pie Pastry: Mix flour and salt in mixing bowl. Cut in shortening with pastry blender until it resembles coarse meal. Add water, tossing with fork to dampen even.

UGLY APPLE DUMPLINGS

1 medium apple
1 pkg. (10 count)
　refrigerated
　biscuits
2 Tbsp. sugar
¼ tsp. cinnamon
2 Tbsp. butter or
　margarine

Remove and discard core from apple. Peel and chop apple. Separate biscuits. On a lightly floured surface, pat or roll each into a 4 inch circle. Place about 1 tablespoon of chopped apple on each biscuit. Stir together the sugar and cinnamon and sprinkle over apple. Dot each with some of the butter. Shape into half moons or bundles. For half moons, moisten edge of biscuits and fold in half over filling. Press down with your fingers or a fork to seal. Place about 2 inches apart on an ungreased baking sheet. Brush with the melted butter. Bake in a 375° oven for 11 to 13 minutes or until golden. Remove to wire rack. Serve warm. Makes 10 servings.

APPLE BREAD PUDDING

1¾ c. milk
½ tsp. vanilla
2 eggs, slightly beaten
2 c. bread cubes or
　chunks
⅔ c. raisins
1 c. brown sugar
3 apples, sliced

Combine milk, vanilla and eggs. Pour over bread in a bowl, and let soften if bread is stale. Add raisins. Sprinkle brown sugar into a buttered 1½ quart baking dish; arrange sliced apples over, pressing slightly into sugar. Pour bread mixture over apples and sugar. Bake at 325° for about 60 minutes or until set.

If desired, the pudding may be inverted so that the apples are on top. To achieve this effect, slide a spatula around the edge of the dish to loosen, and turn the pudding out onto a plate. Yield: 8 servings.

This recipe may be prepared in the top of a double boiler: cook over simmering water for about 1 hour.

EASY CRISPY APPLE DISH

1 (1 lb. 9 oz.) can apple
    pie filling mix
½ c. butter or
    margarine
½ c. brown sugar
½ c. unsifted flour
½ c. quick oatmeal

Place apple filling in a greased 9x9 inch baking dish. In a small pan, melt butter (or margarine) and add brown sugar, flour, and oatmeal. Crumble this mixture on top of apple filling. Bake, uncovered, for 50 minutes at 350°.

OLD-FASHIONED APPLE CRISP

8 large, tart apples,
    peeled and
    sliced
1 tsp. cinnamon
1 c. brown sugar
1 c. granulated sugar
1 c. flour
1 egg
½ tsp. salt
1 tsp. baking powder
½ c. oleo, melted

Place sliced apples in a 9x13 inch baking pan. Combine cinnamon and brown sugar. Sprinkle apples with half of cinnamon and brown sugar mixture. Combine 1 cup granulated sugar, flour, egg, salt, and baking powder. Spread this mixture over apples. This will act as a pie crust dough. Sprinkle remaining cinnamon and brown sugar mixture over dough. Pour melted oleo over the top and bake at 350° for about 40 to 45 minutes.

APPLE-CRANBERRY CRISP

3 c. chopped apples
2 c. raw cranberries
¾ to 1 c. sugar

Topping:
1½ c. oatmeal
½ c. brown sugar
⅓ c. flour
⅓ c. chopped pecans
½ c. melted butter

Combine apples, cranberries, and sugar in an 8 inch square baking dish. Mix thoroughly to blend. Set aside. Combine the topping and mix until crumbly. Spread evenly over the fruit layer. Bake in a 350° oven for 1 hour or until the fruit is fork tender. Serve warm with ice cream or whipped cream. Makes 8 servings.

APPLE BAVARIAN TORTE

Crust:
1 c. flour
⅓ c. sugar
½ tsp. vanilla
½ c. butter

Cheese Filling:
16 oz. cream cheese
½ c. sugar
½ tsp. vanilla
2 eggs (room temperature)

Apple Topping:
2 large tart apples, thinly sliced
¼ c. sugar
½ tsp. cinnamon
½ tsp. vanilla
⅓ c. chopped walnuts

Cut crust ingredients until coarse corn meal. Press onto sides and bottom of 10 inch springform. Bake 5 minutes at 350° or until golden.

Beat cheese, sugar, and vanilla until smooth. Beat eggs in, one at a time. Spoon into cooled crust.

Mix apple topping (except nuts) and spread on top. Sprinkle with nuts. Bake 15 minutes at 450°, then 45 minutes at 350° or until center tester comes clean. Bake crust 15 or 20 minutes until golden.

LAYERED CARAMEL APPLE BISCUIT

2 c. flour
2 Tbsp. sugar
1 Tbsp. baking
 powder
¼ tsp. salt
⅔ c. milk
½ c. margarine,
 melted
1 egg, beaten
28 caramels
¼ c. water
4 c. apple slices
2 c. thawed whipped
 topping with
 real cream

Combine dry ingredients. Add combined milk, margarine, and egg, mixing just until moistened. Bake at 450° for 12 to 15 minutes or until golden brown. Cool 10 minutes; remove from pan. Cool. Split in half horizontally.

Melt caramels with water in heavy saucepan over low heat, stirring frequently until smooth. Add apples; heat. Fill and top biscuit with apple mixture and whipped topping. Serve immediately.

CARAMEL APPLE WALNUT SQUARES

1¾ c. flour
1 c. quick-cooking
 oats
½ c. brown sugar,
 firmly packed
½ tsp. baking soda
½ tsp. salt
1 c. cold margarine or
 butter
1 c. walnuts, chopped
20 caramels
 (unwrapped)
1 (14 oz.) can
 sweetened
 condensed milk
1 (21 oz.) can apple
 filling or topping

Preheat oven to 375°. In large bowl, combine flour, oats, sugar, baking soda, and salt; cut in margarine until crumbly. Reserving 1½ cups crumb mixture, press remainder on bottom of 13x9 inch baking pan. Bake 15 minutes. Add walnuts to reserved crumb mixture.

In heavy saucepan, over low heat, melt caramels with sweetened condensed milk, stirring until smooth. Spoon apple filling over prepared crust; top with caramel mixture, then reserved crumb mixture. Bake 20 minutes or until set. Cool. Serve warm with ice cream. *Delicious!*

DUTCH APPLE DESSERT

¼ c. margarine
1½ c. graham cracker
  crumbs
1 (14 oz.) can
  sweetened
  condensed milk
1 c. (8 oz.) sour cream
¼ c. ReaLemon
  reconstituted
  juice
1 can apple pie filling
¼ c. chopped nuts
½ tsp. cinnamon

Preheat oven to 350°. In a 10x6 inch baking dish, melt margarine. Sprinkle in graham cracker crumbs; stir well. Press to bottom of dish. In medium bowl, stir together the milk, sour cream, and lemon juice. Spread over crumbs. Spoon pie filling over creamy layer. Bake 25 to 30 minutes. Cool slightly. Mix nuts and cinnamon; sprinkle over pie filling.

APPLESAUCE CUSTARD

1 qt. applesauce
1 c. sugar
½ c. flour
2 eggs
2 c. milk
1 tsp. vanilla
1 tsp. butter

Pour applesauce in bottom of baking dish. Mix sugar, flour, eggs, and milk in a pan and bring to a boil. Add vanilla and butter. Pour custard on top of applesauce. Crush 10 double graham crackers and add 4 tablespoons melted butter. Sprinkle over custard. Brown in oven 10 to 15 minutes at 350°. Serves 10.

SOUR CREAM APPLE SQUARES

1¾ c. flour
½ c. flour
2 tsp. baking powder
½ c. butter or
  margarine
2 eggs
1 c. dairy sour cream
1 tsp. vanilla

Apple Filling:
1½ lb. cooking
  apples, peeled,
  cored, and finely
  chopped
½ c. raisins
½ c. sugar
1 tsp. vanilla

Stir together flour, sugar, and baking powder. Cut in butter until pieces resemble small peas. Combine eggs, sour cream, and vanilla; add to flour mixture. Stir until well mixed. Spread half the batter into greased 9x9x2 inch baking pan. Bake at 350° for 15 minutes. Spread apple filling over layer in pan. Carefully spoon remaining batter on top. Bake at 350° for 35 minutes more. Sprinkle with powdered sugar when cooled. Cut into squares. There should be about 16.

FROSTED APPLE SQUARES

Pastry:
2½ c. flour
1 Tbsp. sugar
1 tsp. salt
1 c. shortening
1 egg plus milk to
make ⅔ c.

Filling:
5 c. chopped apple
¼ c. sugar
1 tsp. cinnamon
1 tsp. allspice

Frosting:
1 c. confectioners
sugar
2 Tbsp. lemon juice

Combine flour, sugar, and salt. Cut in shortening and stir in egg and milk. Divide dough in half and roll out each half to a 12x10 inch piece. Place one on a cookie sheet. Spread apples, combined with sugar and spices, over the dough. Place second pastry on top and seal edges. Brush with beaten egg white. Bake at 400° for 40 minutes.

Combine frosting ingredients and drizzle over pastry while still hot. Cut into 16 to 20 squares and serve warm.

APPLE DESSERT

1 can Eagle Brand
milk
¼ c. melted butter
½ tsp. cinnamon
½ tsp. apple pie spice
1 can apple pie filling
½ c. flour
½ c. brown sugar
½ c. coconut
½ c. chopped pecans
2 eggs

Butter 9x9 inch dish. Place pie filling in bottom of dish. Beat eggs. Add milk, butter, cinnamon, and spice; mix and beat. Pour over apples. Mix flour, brown sugar, coconut, and pecans. Cut in ¼ cup oleo and sprinkle over pie filling. Bake at 375° for 45 minutes. Serve hot with vanilla ice cream.

COUNTRY APPLE DESSERT

1 box yellow cake mix
⅓ c. butter, softened
1 egg
1 (20 oz.) can apple
  pie filling
½ c. brown sugar,
  packed
½ c. walnuts, chopped
1 tsp. cinnamon
1 c. sour cream
1 egg
1 tsp. vanilla

Preheat oven to 350°. In a large bowl, combine cake mix, butter, and egg at low speed with electric mixer to form a crumbly dough. Press mixture into bottom of an ungreased 9x13 inch pan. Spread apple pie filling over top. Combine brown sugar, nuts, and cinnamon. Sprinkle over pie filling. Combine sour cream, egg, and vanilla; pour over top. Bake 40 to 55 minutes or until golden brown.

APPLE CINNAMON CRUNCH

1 can pie sliced apples
½ c. butter
1 pkg. apple
  cinnamon cake
  mix
½ c. chopped walnuts
1 tsp. cinnamon

Preheat oven to 350°. Spread apples in a 9 inch square pan. Melt butter in a saucepan; stir in dry cake mix and nuts. Sprinkle over apples. Sprinkle cinnamon over crumb mixture. Bake at 350° for 45 to 50 minutes or until golden brown. Serve with whipped cream.

APPLE PARFAIT DESSERT

1 can apple pie filling
¾ c. quick cooking
  rolled oats
½ c. brown sugar,
  packed
4 Tbsp. margarine
¼ tsp. cinnamon
Vanilla ice cream

In 8x8 inch baking dish, combine oats, brown sugar, butter, and cinnamon. Bake at 350° for 10 minutes. (Mixture will not be crisp.) Let cool and crumble. Layer ice cream, apples, and oatmeal mixture in parfait glasses (or any glass) and serve.

76

APPLE PUMPKIN DESSERTS

1 (21 oz.) can apple
  filling or topping
1 (16 oz.) can pumpkin
  (about 2 c.)
1 (14 oz.) can
  sweetened
  condensed milk
2 eggs
1 c. gingersnap
  crumbs
1 tsp. ground
  cinnamon
½ tsp. ground nutmeg
½ tsp. salt
2 Tbsp. butter, melted

Heat oven to 400°. Spoon apple into 8 to 10 custard cups. In large mixer bowl, beat pumpkin, sweetened condensed milk, eggs, cinnamon, nutmeg, and salt; spoon over apple filling. Combine crumbs and butter. Sprinkle over pumpkin. Place cups on 15x10 inch jelly-roll pan. Bake 10 minutes. Reduce heat to 350°. Bake 15 minutes or until set. Cool. Refrigerate leftovers. Makes 8 to 10 servings.

APPLE BERRY DESSERT

1 large Red Delicious
  apple, cubed
1 large Golden
  Delicious apple, cubed
1 c. fresh sliced
  strawberries
¼ c. chopped toasted
  walnuts
½ c. lemon yogurt
½ c. whipped topping,
  thawed

In a bowl, combine apples, berries, and nuts. Whipped topping and yogurt should be mixed in a large separate bowl. Add the whipped topping mixture into the fruit mixture by folding it in. Cover and chill well.

TRIPLE APPLE DESSERT

1 Tbsp. unflavored
  gelatin
1 Tbsp. sugar
1 c. unsweetened
  apple juice
1 c. unsweetened
  applesauce
1 c. finely diced apples
¼ tsp. almond extract
Apple slices
Mint sprigs

Sprinkle gelatin and sugar over ¼ cup of the apple juice in a small saucepan; let stand 5 minutes to soften. Place over very low heat just until gelatin is dissolved. Stir in remaining ¾ cup apple juice, applesauce, diced apple, and almond extract. Pour into 3 cup mold. Chill until set, about 1 to 1½ hours.

CINNAMON BAKED APPLES

6 large baking apples,
  peeled and
  cored
¼ c. plus 2 Tbsp.
  sugar, divided
1½ tsp. cinnamon,
  divided
1½ tsp. nutmeg,
  divided
2 Tbsp. butter, divided
½ to ¾ c. apple juice
Red food coloring
  (optional)

Place apples in a shallow 2 quart casserole; pour 1 tablespoon sugar into cavity of each apple. Sprinkle each with ¼ teaspoon of cinnamon and nutmeg. Top with 1 teaspoon butter. Place apple juice in a saucepan and bring to a boil. Stir in food coloring if desired. Pour mixture into casserole. Bake, uncovered, at 400° for 50 to 60 minutes or until tender; baste occasionally with juice mixture. Yield: 6 servings.

HONEY-GLAZED APPLES

5 medium size cooking
  apples
2 Tbsp. water
¼ c. honey
⅓ c. firmly packed
  brown sugar
1 Tbsp. butter or
  margarine,
  melted
½ tsp. vanilla extract
⅛ tsp. ground
  cinnamon
Dash of ground
  nutmeg

Cut apples in halves lengthwise; core. Place apples, cut side up, in a large greased 12x8x2 inch baking dish. Add water to dish. Combine remaining ingredients; spoon into the apple cavities. Cover the dish with aluminum foil. Bake at 375° for 25 minutes or until the apples are tender. Yield: 10 servings.

BUTTERSCOTCH APPLES

3 apples
½ c. butter
¾ c. brown sugar
¾ c. bread crumbs
¼ tsp. salt
½ pt. whipping cream

Peel and cut apples in halves; core. Cream ¼ cup of butter with ½ cup sugar; add bread crumbs and salt. Mix well. Put rest of butter in bottom of pan. Sprinkle rest of sugar on this. Lay apples on this with inner side up. Spread bread crumb mixture over apples. Pour hot water in, just enough to cover bottom of pan. Bake for 1 hour in oven at 375°. Whip cream and serve with apples.

CHRISTMAS APPLES

12 to 18 small Red
  Delicious apples
1 c. water
1 c. sugar
2 c. white syrup
1½ tsp. red food
  coloring

Bring syrup mixture to a boil in a Dutch oven. Place peeled and cored apples in boiling mixture; cook over medium heat until apples are tender, but not too soft. Cover to speed cooking time and turn occasionally to tint evenly. (Cooking time: Approximately 30 minutes.) Remove cooked apples from syrup and refrigerate. Use apples to garnish around turkey platter.

These may be used as a salad if stuffed with a cream cheese, date, nut, and celery mixture, or a whipped cream and raisin mixture.

MILK MAID CARAMEL APPLES

1 lb. Milk-Maid
  caramels (allow
  approx. 9 caramels
  per apple)
5 medium red apples
2 Tbsp. water (use a
  measuring spoon)
5 wooden sticks

Wash and dry apples; insert a stick in stem end. Put caramels and water in top of double boiler; cook over hot water, using a very low flame. Stir occasionally as caramels begin to melt (should take approximately 15 minutes for caramels to melt completely). Dip apples into melted caramels. Twirl once or twice until apples are well coated. Spoon caramel sauce on to completely cover apple. Place apples on butter coated wax paper and place in refrigerator until cool.

For extra flavor, roll apple in chopped nuts.

APPLE BROWNIES

2 c. brown sugar
⅔ c. butter
1 tsp. vanilla
2 eggs
½ tsp. salt
2 c. flour
2 tsp. baking powder
1 c. apples, chopped
Powdered sugar

Preheat oven to 350°. Cream brown sugar and butter. Add vanilla and eggs. Mix thoroughly. Add salt, flour, and baking powder. Mix well. Mix in apples. Bake in a greased 9x13 inch pan. Bake for 30 minutes. Let cool and sprinkle with powdered sugar.

APPLE ENCHILADAS

1 can apple pie filling
1 pkg. flour tortillas
1 stick butter
1 c. sugar
1 c. water

Spoon small portions of apple pie filling into flour tortillas. Roll and place in baking dish. Melt butter with sugar and water. Pour over tortillas. Bake at 400° until brown on top.

APPLE CRISP PIZZA

Pastry for a single
  crust pie
⅔ c. sugar
3 Tbsp. all-purpose
  flour
1 tsp. cinnamon
4 medium baking
  apples, peeled
  and cut into ½ inch
  slices

Topping:
½ c. all-purpose flour
⅓ c. brown sugar
⅓ c. rolled oats
1 tsp. cinnamon
¼ c. softened butter or
  margarine
¼ to ½ c. caramel ice
  cream topping or
  caramel apple dip
Vanilla ice cream
  (optional)

Roll pastry to fit a 12 inch pizza pan. Fold the dough under the rim of the pan or flute the edges. Combine the sugar, flour, and cinnamon in a bowl. Add the apples and toss. Arrange the apples in a single layer in a circular pattern to completely cover the pastry. Combine the first 5 topping ingredients and sprinkle over the apples. Bake at 350° for 35 to 40 minutes or until apples are tender. Remove from the oven and immediately drizzle with the caramel topping or dip. Serve warm with ice cream if desired.

APPLE SORBET

2 c. applesauce
1 c. apple juice
2 Tbsp. lemon juice
2 Tbsp. sugar

Combine in a batter bowl, then divide into 3 ice cups. Freeze. Shave into a bowl and scoop into serving cups. Serve with a spoon.

INDEX OF RECIPES

DESSERTS